Reflecting Christ

Reflecting Christ

being

Edited by
Ray E. Barnwell, Sr.

WESLEYAN
PUBLISHING HOUSE
Indianapolis, Indiana

Contributing Writers and Editors

Ray E. Barnwell, Sr.
Joseph Colaw
Lowell E. Jennings
JoAnne Jones
Kelvin Jones
Nancy Nason-Clark
Wayne Schmidt
Darlene Teague
Lawrence W. Wilson
Donald D. Wood
Paul Baker Wood

Discipleship Project Committee

Earle L. Wilson, Chairman
Ray E. Barnwell Sr., Project Director
Martha Blackburn
Dan Berry
Donald D. Cady
Ross DeMerchant
Steve DeNeff
James Dunn
Russ Gunsalus
Ron McClung
Robert Brown, Advisory Member
Darlene Teague, Advisory Member

Table of Contents

Preface

Reflecting Christ. What a worthy desire! It's an awesome privilege for a believer simply to reflect the glory of our Lord.

Unfortunately, many people are more focused on *doing* than on *being*. Since others usually judge us by our ability rather than our character, it's tempting to pour our energy into achievements at the neglect of spiritual vitality. Our culture has lost the true connection—the connection to God through His son, Jesus Christ.

The neglect of the inner life has sad consequences. In a society that is driven by the need to succeed, many wink at the immoral lifestyles and corrupt practices of leaders. They believe that private life—being—has no connection to public life—doing. That deception is prevalent, in part, because of the belief that there is no absolute truth. Our culture questions whether truth exists, and, if it does, whether it's possible to live by it.

Absolute truth does exist! It is found in Jesus Christ. Jesus said, "I am the way and the truth and the life. No one comes to the Father except through me" (John 14:6). Living according to the truth must be the ultimate desire of every fully devoted follower of Christ. This is the goal of discipleship.

The purpose of this book, one in a series of books called *Building Faith,* is to help you reconnect *being* with *doing* in your life—to help you link the inner life of thoughts and beliefs with the outer life of relationships and actions. As you read this book, you'll be challenged to learn more about Christ, to emulate His character, to reflect His holiness—to be Christlike.

Chapter one begins where many people have left off—with the question of control in your life. You will learn what it means to make Christ the Lord of your life, and you'll discover the joy of surrendering yourself completely to Him.

Most of us are searching for joy, fulfillment, and peace, often in the wrong places. The second chapter will direct you to the true source of contentment—the will of God. You'll learn that God has a plan for your life, and you'll learn how to pursue it.

If you were to offer a drink of water to someone who is thirsty, would it make any difference in the world? Yes, it would. As followers of Jesus Christ, we are interested in meeting the ever-present social needs of our world. Chapter three explains why social action is important for every believer.

Leadership is a buzzword these days. Nearly everyone has a plan for motivating and directing other people. Yet Jesus calls us to be servants. In chapter four you'll discover that we reflect Christ best by becoming *servant leaders.*

The Bible teaches that the family is a reflection of the church. Today, powerful forces tear constantly at the basic unit of society—the family. The fifth chapter helps us to understand the value of the family, and our place in it.

To aid us in living holy lives, we explore two important Bible passages in chapter six: the Twenty-third Psalm and John chapters 14–17. These pivotal scriptures explain God's relationship with His people and Jesus' relationship with His followers. Through them, we'll learn the basic ways in which we reflect Christ.

Suffering! What can I learn from that? In fact, suffering is an unavoidable part of life and can be a valuable learning experience. In chapter seven you'll gain a fresh perspective on this universal experience.

The final chapter takes us into the battle—spiritual battle with the enemy. Our understanding of the spiritual affects our very being. Who is the enemy? How can we have victory? We'll find out in this vital chapter.

As you use this book, there is a tool that will help you put it all together—the *Building Faith* Chart. (You'll find it in the Introduction.) You will see that there are ten important truths that form the foundation of every disciple's life. Those truths are woven throughout this book. To help you connect these important principles to your life—and to show you how they function in the church—we've summarized them in the *Building Faith* Chart. You'll want to refer to it often.

Before you turn another page, you may want to take a good look at yourself. You're about to enter a new phase of spiritual development. You many not fully recognize yourself after you've finished *Reflecting Christ: being!*

RAY E. BARNWELL, SR.

Introduction

Welcome to the exciting journey of discipleship! This book—part of the *Building Faith* series—offers a great opportunity for spiritual growth. In fact, the entire series has been developed for just that purpose: to help you grow as a disciple of Jesus Christ. By participating in this study, you will be shaping your life according to God's Word by using spiritual disciplines such as Bible study, prayer, fasting, Scripture memorization, meditation, and journal writing.

The Goal: Building People

Discipleship is the continuing process of spiritual development. It begins at conversion and continues as long as we live—it's a lifelong journey. Our strategy for making disciples is called *Building People*. The *Building People Strategy* is built upon four core values:

- Sharing Love—Evangelism
- Shaping Lives—Discipleship
- Serving Like Christ—Ministering to Society
- Sending Leaders—Mobilization

Here's how it works: having discovered Christ, you will want to grow in your knowledge of Him—shaping your life according to God's Word. As you do, you will discover a personal ministry, a way to use your spiritual gifts to serve others. Then, having been filled with compassion for others, you will be moved to go into the world, fulfilling the Great Commission by evangelizing the lost—thus completing the cycle of discipleship.

The Process: Building Faith

We implement the *Building People Strategy* through a process called *Building Faith*. *Building Faith* is a *competencies model*, meaning that it's focused on integrating important abilities into every aspect of a believer's life. These core competencies are organized around five categories:

- Biblical Beliefs

- Lifestyle Practices

- Virtues

- Core Values

- Mission

This process aims to form disciples according to the *Great Commandment* and the *Great Commission*.

The method is summarized in the chart that follows. You'll want to bookmark this page and refer to it often.

Building Faith				
Foundational Beliefs	**Lifestyle Practices**	**Personal Virtues**	**Core Values**	**Mission**
The Trinity	Worship	Joy	Biblical Authority	Discipling Believers
Salvation by Grace	Prayer and Faith	Peace and Grace	Biblical Authority	Evangelizing the Lost
Authority of the Bible	Practicing the Mind of Christ and Discipline	Faithfulness	Biblical Authority	Discipling Believers; Equipping the Church
Personal Relationship with God	Bible Study and Prayer	Self-Control	Christlikeness; Disciple-Making	Discipling Believers
Identity in Christ	Baptism, Lord's Supper	Humility and Grace	Local Church Centered	Discipling Believers
Church/ Family of God	Biblical Community of Faith Beginning in a Christian Home	Love	Local Church Centered; Servant Leadership	Ministering to Society; Discipling Believers
Eternity/Global Evangelism	Lifestyle Evangelism	Love and Obedience	Disciple-Making; Unity in Diversity	Evangelizing the Lost
Stewardship (Including Good Works, Compassion)	Making Christ Lord of Time, Money, Life	Humility, Patience and Goodness	Disciple-Making; Servant Leadership	Equipping the Church; Ministering to Society
Freedom of the Will	Biblical World View	Obedience	Cultural Relevance; Biblical Authority	Discipling Believers; Equipping the Church
Holiness	Godliness, Loving Obedience to God's Revealed Will	Patience, Gentleness, Kindness, Love	Christlikeness; Disciple-Making	Discipling Believers; Ministering to Society

Foundational Truths

Building Faith is based on ten foundational truths, which are key elements for life transformation. These biblical concepts encompass the scope of Christian thinking. Learning these important concepts will help you grow in the faith.

Practices

Every believer must move from theory to practice. That is, he or she must learn to apply biblical truth to life. The practices identified in *Building Faith* will assist you to enact your faith and will become the evidence of the change that's taken place in your life.

Virtues

Virtues are Christlike qualities that emerge in the life of a believer, replacing sinful thoughts and attitudes. These virtues reveal the developing character of a transformed person and attract others to Christ. These virtues are also known as the *fruit of the Spirit.*

Core Values

Biblical truth must be applied in the framework of Christ's body, the church. The core values are the guiding principles by which the church should function. They are our method of operating, describing *how* we do the things we do.

Mission

Ultimately, believers are called to serve. The mission describes what it is that we do for Christ. Each biblical truth finds a practical expression in our work.

Your Involvement: Spiritual Disciplines

These days, many people who are searching for faith have discovered something exciting in Christian worship. The worship service is the point of entry to most churches. Yet as important as worship is, believers need something more in order to grow in the faith. Most of the new believers I speak with still have questions; they're looking for clarification. And they are longing for Christian relationships. Wouldn't it be great if there was a place you could go to make friends and find answers? Wouldn't it be wonderful if you could discover a forum to open your heart, grow in the faith, and find unconditional love?

There is such a place!

Sunday School and other small group discipleship settings provide exactly that kind of environment for building faith. Discipleship moves beyond worship to involve people in building their faith in the context of loving relationships. Just as the New Testament church was built on teaching and preaching (Acts 5:42), so today's church must be built on Bible study. Gaining a thorough knowledge of the Bible is best done by participating in a Sunday School class or Bible study group in addition to attending worship services. Both are important. One without the other can create an imbalance in your spiritual life. Being connected to a family-like unit that's relationship based is a vital component of discipleship.

In most churches, that caring, nurturing unit is called Sunday School. Other churches achieve this interaction through discipleship groups of various kinds. Whatever the name, day, or place of meeting, the fact is that everyone needs a protected environment in which to discover and practice the faith.

If you want to grow and become more effective in the Christian faith, then I urge you to join a Sunday School class or discipleship group.

Along with involvement in a discipleship class or small group, there are some other simple disciplines that have been proven to enhance spiritual formation. You can boost your spiritual growth by using these simple tools.

Bible Reading and Study

The *Building Faith* series is designed to direct you to the Bible at every point in your study. Each chapter begins with one or two important Scripture passages and includes dozens of Bible references to explore. You can enhance your Bible study by using a good Bible translation, written in today's language, such as the New International Version (NIV).

Scripture Memorization

Memorization is a simple way to gain ownership of important Scripture verses. Each of the chapters in this book includes a key verse to memorize. At the end of the book is a Scripture memory tool—perforated flash cards containing the key verse for each chapter. Use them to memorize these verses and you'll gain confidence in your knowledge of Scripture.

Daily Prayer and Reflection

Time alone with God is perhaps the single most important spiritual practice for any disciple. Spend time in prayer and reflection every day.

Personal Spiritual Journal

Journal writing is a way to enhance time spent in prayer and reflection. Recording observations about your life and faith will help you process what you are learning and clarify the spiritual issues in your life. There is a personal spiritual journal page included in each chapter of this book. At the end of each book is an extended journal section that you may use to expand your journal writing. Take this study as your opportunity to begin the practice of journal writing. You'll be glad you did.

Now, let's get started on the exciting journey of *Building Faith!*

Giving up without a Fight

The Lorship of Christ

> *But our citizenship is in heaven. And we eagerly await a*
> *Savior from there, the Lord Jesus Christ, who, by the power*
> *that enables Him to bring everything under His control, will*
> *transform our lowly bodies so that they will be like His*
> *glorious body.*
>
> —Philippians 3:20–21

 **Bible Basics**

Matthew 6:24

No one can serve two masters. Either he will hate the one and love the other, or he will be devoted to the one and despise the other.

John 1:1–3

¹In the beginning was the Word, and the Word was with God, and the Word was God. ²He was with God in the beginning. ³Through Him all things were made; without Him nothing was made that has been made.

John 11:27

"Yes, Lord," she told Him, "I believe that you are the Christ, the Son of God, who was to come into the world."

Romans 13:14

Rather, clothe yourselves with the Lord Jesus Christ, and do not think about how to gratify the desires of the sinful nature.

Colossians 1:15–20

[15]He is the image of the invisible God, the firstborn over all creation. [16]For by Him all things were created: things in heaven and on earth, visible and invisible, whether thrones or powers or rulers or authorities; all things were created by Him and for Him. [17]He is before all things, and in Him all things hold together. [18]And He is the head of the body, the church; He is the beginning and the firstborn from among the dead, so that in everything He might have the supremacy. [19]For God was pleased to have all His fullness dwell in Him, [20]and through Him to reconcile to Himself all things, whether things on earth or things in heaven, by making peace through His blood, shed on the cross.

Connecting God's Word to Life

List several words that describe Jesus, based on the above Scriptures. Is this description the same or different from what you thought about Jesus before now? How so?

We Are Called to Surrender

The situation seemed hopeless. Encircled by the enemy, low on supplies and ammunition, enduring relentless bombardment and bitter cold, the men of the United States Hundred and First Airborne Division faced starvation or annihilation. It was December 1944. The place was Bastogne, France. The German army had launched the winter offensive that became known as the Battle of the Bulge, overwhelming

American troops in the thinly defended Ardennes forest. Bastogne was surrounded.

At 11:30 A.M. on December 22, the German commander offered American General A. C. McAuliffe a simple proposition: Surrender and live.

What would you have done?

Outnumbered, overmatched, and undersupplied, the American commander shot back a one-word reply that has become a classic symbol of defiance. He said: "Nuts."

Nuts!

That response rallied American troops during the Second World War, and it epitomizes the independent spirit of the modern person. "Nobody tells me what to do. No matter how hopeless the situation, I will be master of my fate. I will never surrender—and *nuts* to anyone who tries to make me!"

> Not even God will compel us do what we choose not to do.

Undeniably, we are free people. God made us that way. We were born with a free will. We are free to accept God's grace or to reject it. Not even God will compel us do what we choose not to do.

Yet that independent attitude, so laudable as a civic principle, produces tragic results as a personal doctrine. Unlike the heroic defenders of Bastogne, those who live by a code of radical individuality may endure bitter consequences. Personal failure, broken relationships, and ruined marriages too often result from a worldview that selfishly asserts "Me first." Freedom becomes slavery for many who are burdened with addictive behaviors, the result of their inability to master their desire to do—or rather not do to—whatever they please.

Into the chaos of our personal freedom, Jesus Christ issues the call to surrender—to surrender our lives to Him, accepting His mastery over the world, the church, and ourselves. Though we are free, He asks that we become servants, accepting His lordship over our lives.

That notion—the lordship of Christ—is challenging for many Christians. We cherish independence as our highest ideal. We're reluctant to surrender our freedom to anyone—an employer, the church, or even Christ Himself.

Yet Christ *is* Lord, and we will live happier and more contented lives if we acknowledge that fact.

Is Christ your Lord? Have you surrendered your life to Him? Let's find out what lordship means why it's so important in our lives.

How important is your freedom? List the areas of your life that you feel sure you'd never surrender to anyone. (Some examples might be career, relationships, or finances.)

Christ Is Lord

It's interesting to read the titles that some political leaders have given themselves. The Queen of England is officially known as Elizabeth II, by the Grace of God, of the United Kingdom of Great Britain and Northern Ireland, and of her other realms and territories Queen, Head of the Commonwealth, Defender of the Faith. Her son is titled His Royal Highness Prince Charles Philip Arthur George, Prince of Wales and Earl of Chester, Duke of Cornwall and Rothesay, Earl of Carrick and Baron Renfrew, Lord of the Isles and Great Steward of Scotland.

Well it *sounds* impressive.

We know, however, that royals now serve a largely ceremonial function. They have grandiose titles but little or no power. They are kings and queens in name only.

That's not true of Jesus. He is Lord in fact as well as in name. He is the Lord of All.

Titles for Jesus	
Scripture	**Title**
Isa. 9:6	Mighty God
Isa. 9:6	Prince of Peace
Isa. 9:6	Everlasting Father
Mark 1:2–3	Lord
Mark 8:29	The Christ
Matt. 26:63–65	Son of God
John 1:1–3	The Word (Is God)
Acts 2:21 (Joel 2:32)	Lord (God)

He Is Lord of Creation

Have you ever thought about how the world was created? We may accept the fact that God did create the world. But how? By what means?

Genesis tells us that God spoke the world into existence. "And God said, 'Let there be light' and there was light" (Gen. 1:3). God created by His Word.

The New Testament tells us more about that. According to John the Apostle, Jesus was the *Word* that created the world. John 1:1–3: "In the beginning was the Word, and the Word was with God, and the Word was God. He was with God in the beginning. Through Him all things were made; without Him nothing was made that has been made."

> Jesus proved He was God's anointed one by His resurrection from the dead.

The Apostle Paul echoes that thought in his letter to Christians at Colossae: "He is the image of the invisible God, the firstborn over all creation. For by Him all things were created: things in heaven and on earth, visible and invisible, whether thrones or powers or rulers or authorities; all things were created by Him and for Him" (Col. 1:15–16).

Jesus, the Word of God, was the agent of creation. He created all that exists.

And there's more. Paul tells us that "He is before all things, and in Him all things hold together" (Col. 1:17). Jesus is also the sustainer of the world. It's He that keeps the world spinning, giving order and purpose to everything that exists.

He Is Lord of Salvation

Jesus is also the *Christ*. Christ, by the way, is a title, not a name. It means "anointed one," and it indicates that Jesus was chosen by God to save the world. This title, derived from the Greek word *christos*, parallels the Old Testament term *messiah*.

The Old Testament predicted that God would send an anointed one to His people (see 1 Sam. 2:35; Ps. 2:2; Dan. 9:25). The New Testament makes it clear that Jesus is that anointed one, the Christ. When Andrew the Apostle met Jesus, he said, "'We have found the Messiah' (that is, the Christ)" (John 1:41). The Apostle Peter preached that "God has made this Jesus, whom you crucified, both Lord and Christ" (Acts 2:36). And Jesus declared Himself to be the Christ (see John 4:25–26).

Jesus was no ordinary person. He was God's anointed one who came to save the world. He proved it by His resurrection from the dead, as the Apostle Paul says in Rom. 1:4: "Through the Spirit of holiness [He] was declared with power to be the

Son of God by His resurrection from the dead: Jesus Christ our Lord."

Because that is true, there is no possibility of salvation without Jesus. Paul wrote: "If you confess with your mouth, 'Jesus is Lord,' and believe in your heart that God raised Him from the dead, you will be saved" (Rom. 10:9). Jesus is God's appointed instrument for bringing salvation to the world. He is the Christ.

Attributes of Jesus	
Scripture	**Attribute**
John 1:1	Eternally Exists
Matt. 28:20	Is Omnipresent
Matt. 28:18	Has Universal Power
Col. 1:16	Created the World
Col. 1:17	Sustains the World
Mark 2:5-7	Has Authority to Forgive
John 20:28	Is Worshiped
John 5:21	Can Raise the Dead
John 5:22, 27	Judges Humankind

He Is Lord of the Church

Although Jesus is now in heaven with the Father, He continues to be our Lord. Paul said that "He is the head of the body, the church; He is the beginning and the firstborn from among the dead, so that in everything He might have the supremacy" (Col. 1:18; see also Eph. 5:23).

Through the power of the Holy Spirit, Jesus the Christ continues to reign over His followers. As His body (the church), we exist in order to serve Him. And as individual Christians, our lives are tied to Him in every way, especially in our hope of eternal life (see especially Rom. 6:1–11). We look forward to the day when He will return to earth for us.

Think of it this way: although we live on earth, we are really citizens of another kingdom, the kingdom of heaven, where Jesus is the ruler. Here's how the Apostle Paul put it in Phil. 2:20–21: "But our citizenship is in heaven. And we eagerly await a Savior from there, the Lord Jesus Christ, who, by the power that enables Him to bring everything under His control, will transform our lowly bodies so that they will be like His glorious body."

Jesus Christ is no paper potentate, a king without a crown. He is Lord of Creation, God's Anointed One, and Lord of the Church. Jesus Christ is truly Lord of all!

How would you translate the term lord into contemporary language? Of the offices, positions, or titles that are used in our society, which ones might fit Jesus?

Christians Accept Christ's Lordship

On July 12, 2001, the government of Yugoslavia gave Alexander Karadjordjevic the use of two palaces in Belgrade, Stari Dvor, the Old Palace, and Beli Dvor, the White Palace. That event marked the first official recognition of the Crown Prince of Yugoslavia in more than sixty years. Born in London in 1945, Alexander is the son of Yugoslavia's last king, Peter II, who fled after Nazi Germany overran the country in 1941. After fifty-one years, the King of Yugoslavia had been invited into his own home.

Other European kings continue to live in exile without official recognition from their home countries. Albania's Leka I was born in 1939 and fled the country with his family three years later. He lives in South Africa. Romania's former King Michael was forced to abdicate his throne in 1947. He lives in Switzerland. Montenegro's Nicolas Petrovic, born in 1944, is heir to the dynasty that ruled that country until the end of World War I. He's an architect living in Paris.

Can you really be a king if you have no kingdom? Does a king need to be crowned, that is, recognized by his people?

Christians do recognize Christ's lordship. We invite Him into the palace of our hearts and crown Him as king of our lives. That takes place in several practical ways.

We Acknowledge Christ's Lordship

The first step in accepting Christ's lordship in our lives is to agree that He is, in fact, the Christ. When Jesus was on earth, many people recognized that truth at a particular moment in their lives. It wasn't uncommon for Jesus Himself to prompt this realization by asking a question or provoking some comment from them.

For example, when Jesus visited the home of Mary and Martha after the death of their brother, Lazarus, Jesus made some startling statements about Himself. Then He asked Martha, "Do you believe this?" Martha said, "Yes, Lord . . . I believe that you are the Christ, the Son of God, who was to come into the world" (John 11:26–27).

On another occasion, Jesus asked the disciples what others were saying about Him. Finally, He asked them directly, "But what about you? . . . Who do you say I am?" Peter answered, "You are the Christ" (Mark 8:29).

At other times, people realized who Jesus was after hearing His teaching or observing Him perform miracles. Even His death led some to accept His lordship. As He died on the cross, one bystander, a Roman centurion, looked on and said, "Surely this man was the son of God!" (Mark 15:39).

Do you believe that Jesus is the Christ? What would it take to convince you that He is?

We Surrender Control

Following the American presidential election of 2000, there was a dispute about who had won. After a close contest, both Al Gore and George W. Bush claimed victory. All attention was focused on Florida, the pivotal state where ballots were counted and lawsuits filed in an attempt to determine the next President of the United States. Finally, Al Gore conceded, surrendering his claim to the office and acknowledging George W. Bush as the new president.

When we accept the fact that Jesus is Lord, we concede control of our lives to Him. We give up our claim to authority.

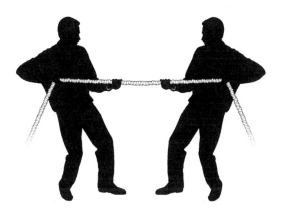

We may fight God for control of our lives

Since we like being master of our own lives, we don't surrender easily. Often, surrendering to Christ does not happen at the moment of conversion. Most people who come to Christ for forgiveness have little thought for the future. Burdened by the guilt of sin, they seek the freedom of forgiveness, and rightly so. They confess their sin and acknowledge Christ as their Savior.

Owning Christ as Lord goes deeper than that. It looks to the future and involves consecrating (setting apart) one's entire life to Him.

Jesus called His disciples to do that when He said, "If anyone would come after me, he must deny himself and take up his cross and follow me" (Mark 8:34). The Apostle Paul testified to that experience when he said, "I have been crucified with Christ and I no longer live, but Christ lives in me" (Gal. 2:20). Those statements portray a person who has given up all claims to his life and is willing to die, even, for the sake of Christ. In fact, the German theologian Dietrich Bonhoeffer put it just that bluntly. He said: "When Jesus Christ calls a man, He bids him come and die."

Making Christ Lord of our lives requires an act of the will that says, "I give up control of my life to Christ. I lay all of my abilities, resources, and plans at His feet. I own Him as my master."

It's tempting to believe that we might share control of our lives with Christ. We certainly want forgiveness from sin and a good relationship with God, but is it really necessary to give *all* of our lives to Christ?

In a word, yes.

Jesus offered simple wisdom with profound meaning when He said, "No one can serve two masters" (Matt. 6:24). Using money as a specific example, He made the point that it's impossible to live for long with divided loyalty. You can't please two bosses. Competing demands will drive a person eventually to serve God or self—never both. Jesus must have first place in our lives, or—as a purely practical matter—He will have none at all.

**You can't please two bosses—
Christ and Self**

Have you consecrated your life to Christ? If so, what led you to make that choice? If not, what is the main obstacle to your surrender?

We Live a New Life

There are some milestones in life that mark dramatic turning points. When you start school, get married, have a baby, or retire, for example, your lifestyle changes dramatically.

Accepting Christ as Lord is like that. Our lives are not the same afterward as they were before. Paul explains that our new life in Christ is just that: a new life. We begin to think and act different. "Therefore, if anyone is in Christ, he is a new creation; the old has gone, the new has come!" (2 Cor. 5:17).

Jesus said, "If anyone loves me, he will obey my teaching. . . . He who does not love me will not obey my teaching" (John 14:23–24). That's pretty clear. If Christ truly is our Lord, then we will give Him authority in our lives. We'll listen to what He says and obey His commands.

So as Christians, we demonstrate that Jesus is our Lord by thinking and behaving in changed ways. We will make it a point to know Jesus' character and to imitate it in our lives.

That change has both negative and positive aspects. On one hand, there are some things that we will avoid. The Bible refers to this as putting off the *old self.* On the other hand, there are new thoughts and behaviors that we'll acquire. The Bible calls that putting on the *new self.* Paul describes that process in Eph. 4:22–24:

> [22]You were taught, with regard to your former way of life, to put off your old self, which is being corrupted by its deceitful desires; [23]to be made new in the attitude of your minds; [24]and to put on the new self, created to be like God in true righteousness and holiness.

The Apostle Peter showed us some practical ways of doing that when he said, "Make every effort to add to your faith goodness; and to goodness, knowledge; and to knowledge, self-control; and to self-control, perseverance; and to perseverance, godliness; and to godliness, brotherly kindness; and to brotherly kindness, love" (2 Pet. 1:5–7). Owning Christ as Lord involves making daily choices that build on the foundation of virtue in our lives. We choose to think and act differently because of our allegiance to Jesus Christ.

The Old Self: Acts of the Sinful Nature Gal. 5:19–21	The New Self: Fruit of the Spirit Gal. 5:22–23
Sexual Immorality	Love
Impurity and Debauchery	Joy
Idolatry and Witchcraft	Peace
Hatred	Patience
Discord and Jealousy	Kindness
Fits of Rage	Goodness
Selfish Ambition	Faithfulness
Dissensions and Factions	Gentleness
Drunkenness and Orgies	Self-Control

Putting off the old self means changing our minds. Paul said, "Clothe yourselves with the Lord Jesus Christ, and do not think about how to gratify the desires of the sinful nature" (Rom. 13:14). We must begin to weave the attitudes and teaching of Jesus Christ into our lives and not allow our minds to dwell on the old ways. That's a process that may take some time.

How is that process going in your life? Are you making progress? These questions may help diagnose the state of your spiritual growth.

- Do I make an effort to know Christ's teaching and obey it?
- Is the old self still in control of some areas of my life?
- Do I ever deliberately ignore God's will in my life?
- Do I think more about what Jesus would do or more about what I want in any situation?
- Can I see growth in my life since acknowledging Christ as Lord?
- Do others see changes in me as a result of Christ's presence in my life?

What is the next change that you need to make in putting off the old self and being obedient to Jesus Christ?

We Trust Him

Have you ever been a passenger in your own car? When someone else is at the wheel, it's hard to keep from offering advice. While it's helpful to rotate drivers on a long trip, we try to get back behind the wheel as quickly as possible. That's especially true if there's heavy traffic, rain, or some other hazard present.

We often do the same thing when it comes to the lordship of Christ. We give control to Him for a while, but when life becomes challenging or painful, we get back behind the wheel.

That's what Peter did when he walked on water to meet Jesus (see Matt. 14:22–32). At first, Peter trusted Jesus and walked toward Him with no problems. But when he saw the wind and the waves, he began to sink.

We often do the same. We trust Christ's lordship when things go smoothly. But when we face job stress, marital trouble, illness, or unhappiness, we forget about Christ and begin to make decisions for ourselves.

Owning Christ as Lord means that we trust Him—all the time.

Jesus taught us to trust God for everything from the food we eat to the clothes we wear. God knows our need and has promised to take care of us (See Matt. 6:25–32). Jesus also promised that He would not desert us (Matt. 28:20; John 14:18) and would send us the *Counselor*, the Holy Spirit, to guide us (John 14:16). When Christ is Lord, we have more security—not less—because He's able to provide for us.

Do you have a tendency to take back control of your life from Christ? What are the situations that cause you to doubt?

Christ's Lordship Brings Contentment

I once visited a restaurant where the dining room was dirty, the service was slow, and the food was lousy. Several months later, I saw a sign at the restaurant that read: "Under New Management." I visited again and found that things had changed. The dining room was sparkling clean, the service was prompt, and I had a delightful meal. New management makes a difference.

That's true in life too. When we surrender our lives to Christ, the "new manager" will make changes for the better. When we surrender control of our lives to Christ, there are good results.

We Have Peace

Peace is a rare commodity in this world. Nations, neighborhoods, workplaces, homes: just about anyplace people are together there's liable to be a fight.

The reason that people can't get along with each other is that they don't have peace with themselves or with God. Since the beginning, our sin has separated us from God and caused trouble in our personal relationships. (See Gen. 3:1–24 to review the ways that sin has affected the world.)

But Jesus brings peace. He said, "Peace I leave with you; my peace I give you" (John 14:27). When He's in control of our lives, we'll be at peace.

That's possible because He has made peace with God for us. Paul wrote, "Since we have been justified through faith, we have peace with God through our Lord Jesus Christ" (Rom. 5:1). Jesus' death atoned for our sin. He made peace with God for us. "For God was pleased to have all His fullness dwell in Him, and through Him to reconcile to Himself all things, whether things on earth or things in heaven, by making peace through His blood, shed on the cross" (Col. 1:19–20).

That means that we're not at odds with God anymore. We have peace with Him, so we can be at peace with ourselves and with others.

In what ways does your attitude about yourself affect your relationships with others?

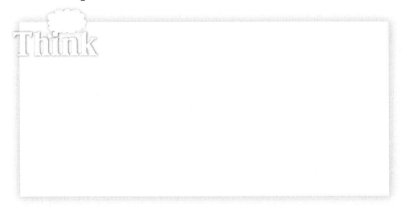

We Have Power

When Christ is in control of your life, you're never truly on your own. You have the power of God at your disposal.

When Jesus went to heaven, He sent the Holy Spirit to His disciples. Through the power of the Spirit, they were enabled to speak the Word of God boldly and perform many miracles (see the book of Acts, especially chapter 2).

That same Holy Spirit is available to all believers in Christ today. The Holy Spirit gives us abilities, or gifts, that we wouldn't otherwise have (see Rom. 12:3–8; 1 Cor. 12:12–31; Eph. 4:10–13).

Although he faced many difficult circumstances in life, including shipwreck, poverty, and imprisonment, the Apostle Paul said, "I can do everything through [Christ] who gives me strength" (Phil. 4:13). When Jesus is Lord, we have the confidence and God-given ability to face the most challenging circumstances.

What are you facing right now or what challenging thing has God called you to do?

We Have Victory

It's ironic. Most of the time, we work very hard at maintaining control of our lives, yet we're almost never successful. In spite of what we'd like to think, we're not very good at controlling our circumstances, or even our own behavior! How often, for instance, have you said, "I wish I hadn't done that," or, "When will I learn to control my temper?"

We probably fail more often than we succeed at managing our lives. The Apostle Paul calls that experience being a "slave to sin" (Rom. 7:14). Without Christ, we're not really in control, even of our own choices.

With Christ in charge, that changes. Through the power of the Holy Spirit living within us, we have freedom from sin and are able to become the people we really want to be. Paul wrote, "Through Christ Jesus the law of the Spirit of life set me free from the law of sin and death" (Rom. 8:2). The Holy Spirit enables us to act on what before were only good intentions.

So in a real sense, we have more freedom when Christ is in control and we're not!

That is sometimes called having *victory* over sin. It's a direct result of accepting Christ's lordship over our lives.

We Have Hope

What happens when you die? Everybody wonders about that, and nearly every religion offers a different view. None of them do much to quell the uneasy feeling that we have when forced to think about the end of life.

Jesus Christ is Lord not only of life but also of death. The Bible says that "He is the beginning and the firstborn from among the dead, so that in everything He might have the supremacy" (Col. 1:18).

> A Christian has no need to fear death. Jesus Christ is Lord—in death and life.

By rising from the dead, Jesus showed that He has conquered it. As Lord of death, He has the power to give life to anyone (see Rom. 6:1–6). That's one of the last messages that He gave to His disciples. Shortly before His own death, Jesus said, "Do not let your hearts be troubled. Trust in God; trust also in me. In my father's house are many rooms; if it were not so, I would have told you. I am going there to prepare a place for you. And if I go and prepare a place for you, I will come back and take you to be with me that you also may be where I am" (John 14:1–3). By trusting Christ with our lives, we gain His promise of eternal life.

As he so often does, the Apostle Paul sums up this incredible hope in Phil. 3:20: "But our citizenship is in heaven. And we eagerly await a Savior from there, the Lord Jesus Christ."

A Christian has no need to fear death. Jesus Christ is Lord—in death and life.

Which Do You Choose?

When you give your life to Christ, you do not lose your autonomy; you gain His authority, power, and help. The result is not slavery, but freedom to enjoy life for the first time.

Bruce Larson, working in New York City, often counseled people facing difficult spiritual decisions. In his book *Believe and Belong,* he tells that he often invites them to stroll to the RCA Building on Fifth Avenue and observe the gigantic statue in the lobby. It depicts Atlas, the Greek god who supposedly carried the world on his shoulders. The statue is of a powerfully built man, but one struggling under an incredible burden. "Now that's one way to live," Larson would point out, "trying to carry the world on your shoulders."

Strolling across the street, he would take the troubled friend to visit a church, where different sculpture offers another approach to life. Behind the altar at Saint Patrick's Cathedral is an image of the boy Jesus, who, with no effort at all, holds the world in the palm of His hand.

When we try to control our own lives the results can be frustrating. We lack peace. We fear death. We carry a world of problems all by ourselves. When Jesus is Lord, we have peace. The power of God is available to us. We are released from guilt and fear.

Which do you choose?

Who is the lord of your life?

 **To Learn More**

Growing Season edited by Stephen M. Miller

More Than Forgiveness by Steve DeNeff

The Four Spiritual Laws booklet by Bill Bright

All additional books and resources are available from Wesleyan Publishing House at www.wesleyan.org/wph or by calling 800.4.WESLEY (800.493.7539).

Personal Spiritual Journal

DATE _____

_____

_____

_____

_____

_____

_____

_____

_____

_____

_____

_____

_____

_____

_____

My Prayer Today—

_____

_____

_____

_____

A Wonderful Plan for Your Life

God's Will

Therefore, I urge you, brothers, in view of God's mercy, to offer your bodies as living sacrifices, holy and pleasing to God—this is your spiritual act of worship. Do not conform any longer to the pattern of this world, but be transformed by the renewing of your mind. Then you will be able to test and approve what God's will is—his good, pleasing and perfect will.

—Romans 12:1–2

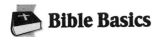 **Bible Basics**

Romans 12:1–2

[1]Therefore, I urge you, brothers, in view of God's mercy, to offer your bodies as living sacrifices, holy and pleasing to God—this is your spiritual act of worship. [2]Do not conform any longer to the pattern of this world, but be transformed by the renewing of your mind. Then you will be able to test and approve what God's will is—his good, pleasing and perfect will.

Colossians 4:12

Epaphras, who is one of you and a servant of Christ Jesus, sends greetings. He is always wrestling in prayer for you, that you may stand firm in all the will of God, mature and fully assured.

Connecting God's Word to Life

Do you know God's will for your life? How would you find out according to Rom.12:1–2?

A Plan for Your Life

Have you ever heard someone say, "God has a plan for your life"? You might have responded with a bit of sarcasm, saying, "Yeah, sure!" Or perhaps you were intrigued by the idea that the Almighty God has thought specifically about you.

Frankly, the phrase "God's will" is used so freely that most people pay it little attention. Can it be true that God does have a plan for *your* life? And if He does, how can you know what it is?

As a beginning point, let's understand that God has a general will for all people. There are some things that He desires for every human being. Beyond that, you can learn to discover His specific will *for you.*

Let's find out how.

Knowing God's General Will

Understanding God's plan for your life begins with some basics. There are some things that God desires for all people. When you understand these, you'll be on your way to discovering God's plan for your entire life.

Salvation

The first and most important element of God's plan for your life is salvation. The Bible declares that God does not want anyone to die in their sins but that everyone be saved through faith in Jesus Christ (2 Pet. 3:9).

How did you come to know Jesus as your Savior?

Holiness

Not only does God want everyone to be saved from the penalty for sin, He also wants every Christian to be saved from the power of sin so that they can live in a way that brings glory to Him (1 Cor. 10:31). God desires for you to do more than simply ask to be forgiven for past sins. He wants to break the power of sin in your life.

It is important for everyone believer to understand that growing Christians should glorify God in everything they do. Whether going to school, working, playing, shopping, interacting in the family, serving in the community, or whatever it might be, Christians are to live every day for God's glory.

Service

The Apostle Peter once wrote to a group of Christians saying that they were "chosen" to be a "royal priesthood" of people who were to declare the praises of God (1 Pet. 2:5, 9). From this we learn that God wants all believers to serve Him in whatever we do, telling people about Christ.

My wife and I have two sons, and our oldest has accepted the call of God to be a pastor. His "call" was a very distinct spiritual experience that led him to believe that God's specific will for him included full-time Christian service.

Our second son, however, felt no such specific call. He would often say, "Dad, I want to serve God, but I don't want to be a preacher!" He, like so many people, had the idea that he could not serve God wholeheartedly unless he entered some vocational ministry, like the pastorate, youth ministry, or cross-cultural missions.

After some discussion, however, he came to understand the biblical concept of the priesthood of all believers (1 Pet. 2:5, 9). He came to see that every believer is in "full-time" service to God and should be engaged in telling others about the good changes that knowing Christ makes in a person's life. He realized that he did not have to be a pastor or missionary to be a be a "priest" for God everyday.

Our second son is now living in a major city and working as a personal fitness trainer. He trains about forty people per week, including retirees, police officers, doctors, business executives, dancers, and professional athletes. He sees new clients every week, bringing him constantly into contact new faces and new professions. He frequently has opportunities to tell clients how his life has been changed by Jesus Christ ("declaring the praises of him who called you out of darkness into his wonderful light," 1 Pet. 2:9). Recently, he said to me, "Dad, I get to share Christ with more people in one week than you do in a year. It's true, I can serve God without being a preacher."

It is God's will for every one of us to be priests who give Him glory, regardless of the profession we may choose.

List three people who are not in vocational Christian ministry but are everyday "priests" to God.

Finding God's Specific Will

Once we understand the basics of God's plan for our lives we can move on to discover His specific will for our lives. One day, Jesus taught His disciples to pray. He used a model prayer that included a plea for God's will to be done here on earth (Matt. 6:10).

Since Jesus told us to pray that God's will be done, it is fair to believe that God does have a specific will, and that includes each one of us. The big question is "How can I know God's plan for my life?" Beyond the general will of God revealed in Scripture, how can I be sure of God's specific will for *my* life?

Most maturing Christians would say that God uses clear principles and patterns when communicating with people. If His Word, the Bible, is silent about some specific issue, we may follow proven biblical principles and patterns as a guide. Here are eight questions that reveal principles for discerning the specific will of God. Your answers to these questions will probably point you in the right direction.

One: Am I Fully Surrendered to God?

The first question concerns your commitment to knowing God and doing His will. Are you fully surrendered to God? Have you allowed Jesus Christ to become Lord of your life, and are you willing to do whatever He wants you to do (Luke 9:23; Gal. 2:20)? Divine leadership comes from Divine presence, so if you have not fully surrendered yourself to God and are not enjoying His active presence in your life, you probably won't be able to discern

> The Holy Spirit brings the presence of God into the life of every believer.

what His will is. The Holy Spirit brings the presence of God into the life of every believer. God's Holy Spirit will guide you into all truth if you are fully surrendered to Him (John 14:15, 17, 25–26; 16:12–15).

Two: Have I Studied the Bible?

If you want to know God, a good place to start is with His Word, the Bible. Have you studied the Bible to become acquainted with God? What principles, commands, or prohibitions do you see in Scripture that might guide you in your search for God's will (Ps. 119:105, 130)? Have you discovered any promises or motivating verses on the subject? If you believe that you know God's will for your life, do you see support for it in God's Word? Study the Bible to help you understand God's will. And be fair in your use of Scripture. Don't pick out only those particular verses that seem to support your own desires. Let God's Word speak for itself.

Three: Have I Prayed about It?

Many people do everything to discover God's will except ask Him. They listen to preachers, read books, and seek inspiration from a variety of sources, but they fail to get alone with God and ask Him. The Bible is filled with stories of people who asked God for specific answers and received them. If you want to know God's will for your life, ask Him (Phil. 4:6).

When you pray, take time to be quiet and listen for an answer from God. Shut off the television, radio, MP3 player, and computer and spend some time with God. Try it for even a brief period of time. Talk to God, then listen for His voice.

You may be wondering, "How will I know if it's God's voice that I'm hearing?" Martin Wells Knapp wrote a wonderful booklet in 1892 to answer that question. Knapp indicated four key elements for testing our impressions to see if they are the voice of God.

> God's leadership always matches biblical truth. That's why it's important for every believer to know the Bible.

Does it Match Biblical Truth? First, is the impression in agreement with Scripture, or does it contradict Scripture? God's leadership always matches biblical truth. That's why it's important for every believer to know the Bible. If you do not know the Bible, then you have no yardstick for telling whether your impressions measure up against God's known will.

Is it the Right Thing to Do? Knapp wrote: "Impressions which are from God are always right. They may be contrary to our feelings, our prejudices and our natural inclinations, but they are always right" (Martin Wells Knapp, Revivalist Publishing, 1892). Some of what we need to consider is simple common sense. Does this promote God and godly principles, or is it selfish or worldly?

Are There Providential Circumstances that Support This Impression? When God is leading, He goes before us and opens doors that make possible that which seems impossible. If your impression is truly God's will, you can expect opportunities to arise that will enable you to proceed with it. Does it appear that God is working to bring about what you feel called to do?

Is it a Reasonable Thing to Do? What is reasonable is sometimes hard to define. When a young woman tells her parents that God has called her to be a missionary in some foreign country, her parents may not think it is reasonable. However, one might look past the emotional response of loving parents to ask, "Has God ever called others to do something similar? Has it succeeded?" Ask yourself and others, "Does my impression sound reasonable? Does it seem to be a likely thing, given my gifts and abilities?"

Four: Does It Match My God-given Gifts and Abilities?

If you can't throw a baseball more than twenty feet but you think God may want you to play for the New York Yankees, it's safe to say that you are not in tune with the will of God. However, if you find that friends constantly ask your advice about their difficulties and you find great fulfillment in encouraging them, your experience and abilities would confirm that your growing desire to be a counselor is God's will for your life. God has uniquely gifted each of us, and He did that so we could find fulfillment in using our abilities to serve Him (1 Cor. 12:4–6).

Five: Does the Holy Spirit Bring This to Mind Continually?

When you pray and visit with other Christians, do you seem continually drawn toward a particular issue, or does your impression seem to grow weaker with time? If what you desire to do is from God, His Holy Spirit will constantly bring your mind back to it. You will have a growing conviction that it is something you must do.

Six: What Is the Advice of Mature Christians on This Issue?

Mature Christians who have had many years of experiencing God's leadership are a wonderful resource for sorting through the myriad options to find God's specific will. The Bible tells us to listen to and accept advice because it will make us wise (Prov. 19:20).

Seven: Do I Have Peace about This Issue?

A sense of peace generally accompanies the will of God. Do you have inner peace about the issue as you pray and take counsel from wise Christians? Or, does the discussion of this issue create a spirit of turmoil for you (Col. 3:15; Phil. 4:6–7)? Something may be good and godly but simply not the right thing for you. When you arrive at God's will, you will have peace.

> If what you desire to do is from God, His Holy Spirit will constatnly bring your mind back to it.

Eight: Is This the Right Time?

God is perfect and His timing is always perfect too. Ask yourself whether you are pushing the issue under your own time schedule or allowing God to work in His own time. Or, are you holding back too long before stepping out? If you are moving on God's schedule, things will tend to fall into place (Ps. 27:14; Lam. 3:26; 2 Cor. 8:11).

If you are trying to discover God's will for your life, you may want to write these questions and spend some time pondering them in the presence of God. After a time of personal worship, consider each question, asking God to speak to you. If the issue at hand is an emotional one, give greater weight to the more objective questions—those that don't rely heavily on personal feelings or opinions.

Discerning God's Will for My Life	
Question	**What God Is Saying about It**
Am I fully surrendered to God?	
Have I studied the Bible?	
Have I prayed about the issue?	
Does this match my God-given gifts and abilities?	
Is the Holy Spirit bringing this issue back time and time again?	
How do mature, godly Christians counsel me regarding this issue?	
Do I have peace about this issue?	
Is this the right time?	

Frequently Asked Questions about God's Will

Discerning God's will is not a black-and-white issue. Few subjects raise more questions in a growing believer's mind. Yet it is possible to know God and to sense His personal will. The responses to these common questions may help you to understand the process of discerning the will of God.

Does God Ever Reveal His Will by Spectacular Means?

Yes. The Bible shows us that God has revealed His will through some amazing methods. The amazing story of Paul's conversion is one example (see Acts 9). The Apostle Peter's incredible vision is another (see Acts 10). Today, there are many Christians who report spectacular revelations of God's will.

It's important to note, however, that these are exceptional happenings. God usually doesn't reveal Himself in extraordinary ways. If God knows that we need miraculous guidance, He will surely give it. Yet it's best to concentrate our attention on learning to discern and discover His will through more common, usual means.

Are People Really Called to Full-time Christian Ministry?

Yes. Not every Christian is called to vocational Christian service—that is, to work as a pastor, missionary, or other Christian occupation. Yet God does call some people to serve Him as a full-time job. People around us will not come to know Jesus unless some of us are willing to go and tell them (Rom. 10:12–15).

Marks of a Calling. If you are wondering whether or not you are called to vocational ministry, there are some basic principles that may guide your decision. John Wesley identified three "marks" that are evident in a person whom God called to vocational ministry.

One is *grace*. Is the person converted? Does he or she display the fruit of the Spirit by living a holy life?

The second mark is *gifts*. That refers to the gifts of the Spirit. Does the person have the ability to understand, reason, speak, communicate, and provide loving care and leadership.

Fruit is the third mark. This refers to the person's effectiveness in ministry. Do people come to know Christ and grow as a result of this person's influence?

When these three marks are evident, the person will likely also have an abiding sense of a divine call that will motivate him or her to full-time Christian vocational service.

> If God gives you a task, He will also give you the ability to do it.

Assessing Your Call. If you feel that you may be called to the ministry, look at these areas of your life to help confirm that calling. First, examine your gifts. If God is calling you to full-time Christian service, He will put within you the spiritual gifts and natural talents that support such a calling. Do your gifts and talents compliment what you believe God is asking you to do?

Many people do not know what their spiritual gifts are. Therefore it's difficult to make an assessment about what they may be called to do. If you are unsure of your spiritual gifts, seek the advice of your pastor. You may also with to complete a spiritual gifts assessment inventory. If you are called to ministry, your spiritual gifts will support and compliment that vocation. (See Rom. 12:6–8; 1 Cor. 12:8–11, 28,

29–31; and Eph. 4:11–12 for more information on spiritual gifts. Also see the resources listed at the end of this chapter.)

Second, if you are called to ministry, it's likely that mature Christians around you will affirm that impression. Do other Christians ask you to share your testimony because when you do it something good often seems to happen? Do other Christians pursue you for counsel because you seem to have a keen insight into God's Word? God nearly always uses spiritually mature Christians to affirm the call.

The third area to examine when assessing your call to ministry is your personal interest. Is this something you want to do? Do you enjoy and find fulfillment in helping others discover the truth about God? Do you delight in studying the Bible? Do you find fulfillment in helping others? Your calling will likely relate directly to the things that you enjoy and find fulfilling.

What factors lead you to believe that you are—or are not— called to vocational Christian ministry?

Can I Miss God's Will for My Life?

Unfortunately, the answer is yes. God's will begins with salvation, and a person may reject God's gracious offer of forgiveness. Beyond that, God's will includes living your life with God in mind—living every day to His glory—and some people, even Christians, focus more on themselves than on God.

In the same way, it's possible to miss God's specific will for our lives. People like King Saul and Jonah are examples of this. Their disobedience caused them either to stray away from God's will or to miss it entirely. Disobedience will affect us in the same way. Any one of us may miss God's will if we begin to tolerate sin in our lives.

It's important to note that people generally do not miss God's will because they don't know what it is. They miss the will of God because they choose not to obey it.

The reason this is possible is that we have a will of our own. We have the freedom to make choices—God made us that way. As we use that freedom to respond to the Holy Spirit's leading, we are able to bring great glory to God. However, if we are swayed by personal, selfish desires, we may choose to do something other than God's will.

Obedience, therefore, is the most important factor for staying in tune with the will of God. And obedience is done one step at a time. Step-by-step, we *can* walk in God's will.

Do you believe that you have discovered the will of God for your life? What will you do to find it?

To Learn More

Follow the Leader by Norman G. Wilson

The Keys for Positive Relationships

Mirror Image edited by Everett Leadingham

The Mystery of God's Will by Charles R. Swindoll

People Just Like Us by Norman G. Wilson

Spiritual Gifts Inventory by Larry Gilbert

All additional books and resources are available from Wesleyan Publishing House at www.wesleyan.org/wph or by calling 800.4.WESLEY (800.493.7539).

Personal Spiritual Journal

DATE _____

_____

_____

_____

_____

_____

_____

_____

_____

_____

_____

_____

_____

_____

My Prayer Today—

_____

_____

_____

_____

CHAPTER 3

A Cup of Cold Water

Social Issues

If anyone has material possessions and sees his brother in need but has no pity on him, how can the love of God be in him? Dear children, let us not love with words or tongue but with actions and in truth.

—1 John 3:17–18

 **Bible Basics**

Matthew 25:31–40

[31]When the Son of Man comes in his glory, and all the angels with him, he will sit on his throne in heavenly glory. [32]All the nations will be gathered before him, and he will separate the people one from another as a shepherd separates the sheep from the goats. [33]He will put the sheep on his right and the goats on his left. [34]Then the King will say to those on his right, "Come, you who are blessed by my Father; take your inheritance, the kingdom prepared for you since the creation of the world. [35]For I was hungry and you gave me something to eat, I was thirsty and you gave me something to drink, I was a stranger and you invited me in, [36]I needed clothes and you clothed me, I was sick and you looked after me, I was in prison and you came to visit me." [37]Then the righteous will answer him, "Lord, when did we see you hungry and feed you, or thirsty and give you something to drink? [38]When did we see you a stranger and invite you in, or needing clothes and clothe you? [39]When

did we see you sick or in prison and go to visit you?" [40]The King will reply, "I tell you the truth, whatever you did for one of the least of these brothers of mine, you did for me."

Connecting God's Word to Life

In this Scripture, observe the various ways a person might serve God by serving others. List some things you could do to serve God by serving those in need.

Compassion is Love in Action

In cities of the developing world, one out of every four households lives in poverty.[1]

Six million children die each year in developing nations from hunger-related causes.[2]

The adult HIV prevalence rate in South Africa in 1999 was 19.9 percent.[3]

In the United States, there are nearly three times as many animal shelters as there are shelters for battered women and their dependent children.[4]

Around the world, almost 246 million children between the ages of five and seventeen work instead of attending school.[5]

The United Nations estimates that 180 million people worldwide consumed illegal drugs in the 1990s. Of these, 9 million were addicted to heroin.[6]

It is estimated that 760 thousand people are homeless on any given night in the United States and from 1.2 to 2 million people are homeless during any one-year period.[7]

Domestic violence is a leading cause of injury and death to women worldwide.[8]

As Christians, you and I are asked to offer a cup of cold water in the name of

Christ. That sounds simple, but sometimes it can be challenging.

What did Jesus mean by "water"?

Who is to offer it?

Who will provide it?

Who is responsible to take it?

Should a committee be formed?

What form of transportation is best?

Will training be required?

What if one cup leads to a request for an endless supply?

A Pharisee once posed a similar question when he asked Jesus "Who is my neighbor?" The question was meant to clearly define his responsibility for obeying the biblical command to "love your neighbor as yourself" (see Lev. 19:18 and Luke 10:27). In response, Jesus narrated the familiar story of the Good Samaritan. The neighbor in the story was the Samaritan, the one who saw the need and was willing to meet it. The point of Jesus' story was that every person in need is our neighbor. Jesus' pointed command to "go and do likewise" makes it clear that we have a responsibility to show compassion to those around us who are in need (Luke 10:40).

> Compassion is love in action. It is doing what we say and living what we believe.

When we hear the command of Christ, we must respond. When Jesus called Andrew and Peter, they laid down their nets and followed. When God called Priscilla and Aquilla, they pulled up stakes and moved to Ephesus. When God called Noah, he built an ark. What then are we to do in response to Jesus' command to "go and do likewise"? We must offer ourselves as a living sacrifice, holy and pleasing to God—this is our spiritual act of worship (Rom. 12:1). God so loved that He gave (John 3:16). We, too, must respond compassionately, giving to those in need.

Simply put, compassion is love in action. It is doing what we say and living what we believe. Compassion is a choice. It begins with individual acts of human kindness and becomes, by the Spirit of the Living God, a way of life.

What needs do you see in your family, church, or community?

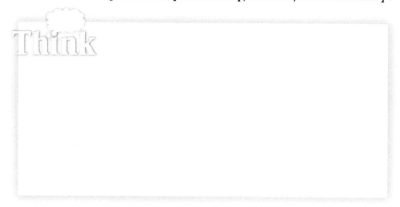

Examples of Love in Action

There are many Bible stories that reveal acts of compassion. Here are four examples of people who saw a need and acted upon it.

Selected Biblical Stories of Compassion				
Who	**Where**	**Need Identified**	**Compassionate Action**	**Scripture**
Dorcas	Her Home	Widows Without Adequate Clothing	Sewing Clothing	Acts 9:35–42
Friends of the Paralytic	A Crowded House	Sick Friend	Bearing a Stretcher to Jesus	Mark 2:1–5
Large Crowd	Leaving Jericho	Blind Beggar	Calling for Attention	Mark 10:46–52
Good Samaritan	On the Roadway	Injured Traveler	Provision of Transportation and Medical Care	Luke 10:30–37

Dorcas

Dorcas was an old woman who made a living as a seamstress in her tiny upstairs apartment. She was well known for her love of Christ and her help of the poor. With a needle and some thread, she responded to the needs of widows who were without adequate clothing. Dorcas is the only disciple that we know of who was brought back to life due to an urgent request from believing community. Her nimble fingers and the crude tools that she used were indispensable to the ministry of the church at Joppa. Dorcas was in the habit of giving her time and energy to help others.

Friends of the Paralytic

Once, there were four men who had a very sick friend. They heard that Jesus was teaching in a nearby home so they carried their friend there on a stretcher. When they arrived, the house was so crowded that they could not get inside. Undeterred, the four men simply carried the stretcher onto the roof, dug through it, and lowered their sick friend to Jesus. These unnamed men were determined to overcome any obstacle to help their friend.

> When we see a need, we should do something practical about it

Bartimaeus

Bartimaeus was a blind man who sat begging beside the road near Jericho. As Jesus was passing by one day, the beggar called out for help. Interestingly, the first response of the crowd was to urge the man to be quiet. They didn't want the disruptive beggar to disturb Jesus. Then Jesus stopped and asked the crowd to call the beggar to him. The crowd responded. "Cheer up! On your feet! He's calling you." Bartimaeus cast aside his only possession, a cloak, jumped to his feet, and went to Jesus, who restored his sight. The crowd overcame their initial reluctance and helped the blind beggar find healing.

The Good Samaritan

The Samaritan in Jesus' often-told story was someone who had the courage to respond to a desperate need. Unlike the two "religious" people in the story—a Levite and a priest—the Samaritan did not look the other way when he came upon a traveler who had been beaten and robbed. He bandaged the man's wounds and transported him to an inn to receive further care—and the Samaritan paid the cost himself. The Good Samaritan was willing to become involved in the life of a stranger, doing what he could to meet a very desperate need.

Dorcas and the Samaritan remind us that we are called to act—at least initially—on our own. When we see a need, we should do something practical about it. The friends of the paralytic show that it often takes the cooperation of several people to meet a need. What one could not do on his own, they accomplished together. The miraculous healing of Bartimaeus demonstrates that our first reaction to a situation may not be the right one. When God opens our eyes to the true need, we must respond.

Seeing the needs of others, in our families, churches, communities, and indeed around the world is not always easy. Often, like the crowd that surrounded

Bartimaeus, we are blinded to the suffering of others and the role we might play in relieving it. Just as new Christians need to learn to how to study the Bible and talk to God, so growing disciples must be taught how to recognize suffering and show compassion within—and beyond—the walls of their own churches.

What is your first reaction when confronted with the need of another person? Why do you respond as you do?

Believers as Salt and Light

In Jesus' Sermon on the Mount, He told the crowd assembled on the hillside that they were the "salt of the earth" (Matt. 5:13). Those who make their living fishing sometimes "salt the catch" to prevent the raw fish from spoiling. By doing so, they extend the shelf life of the fish and provide food to hungry people who may live a great distance from the sea. Salt has a number of uses, and they illustrate the role that we Christians are to play in a needy world.

Christians are sacred salt when we—
• **Bind up the wounds of others.** • **Make the rough pathway smooth.** • **Bring out the pleasing aspects of others' character.** • **Act as a preservative in the world.**

Sacred Salt

Salt has a medicinal quality in that it promotes healing. As we serve others, we will bind up their wounds, applying the healing balm of Gilead (Jer. 8:22) to their ailments and their disappointments. Salt also acts as a deicer. In winter weather, applying salt to walkways makes the treacherous path safe. In the same way, we sometimes help to smooth over the rough spots in others' lives.

Why do most of us like potato chips or French fries so much? It's because salt enhances the flavor of the potatoes. When we invest time in the lives of others, we build up their self-esteem, help them to recognize their unique value, and prompt them to think about serving others. We, too, add flavor to the world by enhancing the attractiveness of others.

Also, salt is a preservative. Through our acts of kindness we can insulate others from pain and suffering. As a seatbelt helps to protect a car passenger, we can help to protect someone else from danger or further harm. Each time a Christian volunteers at a soup kitchen, takes toiletry supplies to a transition house or groceries to a food bank, he or she is acting as sacred salt—a preservative in a decaying world.

Divine Light

Jesus also said that we should let the light of our lives shine forth to brighten the darkness caused by pain, loneliness, and despair. How do we do this?

> ### Christians are divine light when we—
>
> - **Point others toward the light of Christ.**
> - **Reflect His light by our words and actions.**
> - **Draw energy from the light of the gospel.**
> - **Offer warmth to those around us.**

Jesus observed that a light set upon a hill illuminates the entire village while one hidden in a barrel does nothing. By what we say and do as believers, we let our light shine to point others toward the light of Christ. We may do that intentionally, as when we are invited to tell someone about our experience. More often, perhaps, we shine unknowingly when others observe our behavior and see the light of Christ. Whenever we point to Christ, we draw attention away from ourselves. Although our individual lights may be dim, the light of Christ shines brightly through us.

Christians not only point to the light, but they reflect it as well. The good things we do reveal to others the source of our strength and the reason for our determination. Since no believer is strong enough to rely on his or her own resources alone, we can draw energy from the Word of God. The psalm writer said,

"Thy word is a lamp unto my feet and a light unto my path. . ." (Ps. 119:105, KJV).

By pointing others to the Light and reflecting that same Light in our lives, we offer warmth to those around us. There are many times when our world seems cold and impersonal, and the load that a neighbor has to bear is too great. By pointing to the Light—Christ—and reflecting its rays, we make another person's journey a bit easier. God's Spirit will lead us as we reveal more of the Light, and the chorus of saints who have already won the race will cheer us on (Heb. 12:1).

Principles for Compassionate Action

Social action requires more than just the motivation to do good. In fact, good intentions alone sometimes bring more harm than good. When faced with the challenge of assisting with a personal or social need, we must be able to understand the problem and to accurately assess the forms of help that might be needed. Here are some guiding principles for compassionate action.

Guiding Principles for Showing Compassion
. **Know the facts.** . **Interpret the facts in context.** . **Ask what help is needed.** . **Assess your ability to help.** . **Offer assistance, not control.**

Know the Facts

Clearly, knowing the facts is a first step. Listed below and at the beginning of this chapter are a variety of world issues.

- According to the World Health Organization, one in five women around the globe will be physically or sexually abused during her lifetime.[9]
- More than one million children are forced into prostitution each year. The majority of them live in Asia.[10]
- It is estimated that there are approximately 3.6 physicians in Kenya for every 100 thousand people and 2.2 dentists per 100 thousand people.[11]
- Female genital mutilation, or female circumcision, is practiced in as many as 28 African countries and in at least two countries outside of Africa.[12]
- More than 800 million people in the world are hungry.[13]

- It is estimated that 25 thousand women are victims of rape each year in Peru, most of them younger than fourteen years of age.[14]
- The literacy rate for Haiti is 45 percent; for Niger 13.6 percent; for Canada 97 percent.[15]

Knowing the facts is the first step toward compassionate action. When we see the needs that exist, we will be motivated to act.

Interpret Facts in Context

Facts, without a broader base of knowledge for understanding them, can lead either to a sense of confusion or apathy. Facts must be interpreted in context. To do that, it will be useful to consult a variety of credible sources that represent different perspectives.

For example, consider the issue of human trafficking. How prevalent is this problem? What are the countries of origin for women and children sold into slavery? Who are the consumers? How are these operations financed? Why does human trafficking often go undetected? What eventually happens to a young woman

> We need to know the facts, but we must interpret those facts in context.

who is lured from an Asian country to North America with the promise of a job, only to be forced into prostitution? What level of desperation in the sending country drives this problem? What are the problems with helping someone to escape? What is the role of legislation in solving this global problem?

Obviously, there are many factors contributing to this problem. It is driven by the poverty and lack of access to employment that many women face in developing nations. It is also fueled by greed and the desire for sex on demand in developed countries, as well as sleeping governments that turn a blind eye to the problem.

To eradicate this complex problem would require simultaneous intervention at several levels. Women and children freed from forced prostitution would need a variety of social services. Increased international law enforcement and economic development in the countries of origin would be needed to prevent further trafficking.

Thus, we need to know the facts in order to be motivated to meet a need, whether it is poverty, sexual assault, child abuse, illiteracy, or disease. But in order to form a response we must interpret those facts in context.

Ask What Help Is Needed

Once we understand the problem in context, we are in a position to ask appropriate questions about what help is needed. What would solve the problem? What resources are needed? What underlying causes need to be addressed? How might that be done?

Assess Our Ability to Help

Then, we can assess our own ability to offer assistance. What resources are available? What can we offer and for what period of time?

Offer Assistance, not Control

Remember that there is a fine line between offering assistance and assuming control. In the parable of the Good Samaritan, the Samaritan provided transportation and paid for extended care for the injured traveler. We are not told that the Good Samaritan lectured the unfortunate victim on the dangers of the highway. Nor did the Good Samaritan take over the traveler's decision making. Through this parable, Jesus taught that when a need is presented, the compassionate neighbor assesses what he or she can do to help and then does it promptly.

> By acting compassionately, we *can* make a difference in the world. The question is, why don't we?

Motivation to Act

Many people are making a difference in the world. Organizations like World Hope International are working to bring relief to serious problems in many countries of the world. In North America, many congregations are working to meet the needs of those around them.

And many are not.

If the hallmark of the Christian community is love, then the obvious result of congregational life should be caring for one another and our world. The question for each of us is: What does it mean to show love in the neighborhood where I live, the office where I work, or the church I attend? By acting compassionately, you and I *can* make a difference in the world. The question is, why don't we?

There are at least three reasons.

We Lack Vision

Late one spring, I visited Croatia—a nation and a people who are no stranger to violence, despair, and struggle. The constant fighting there has left many children orphans.

While there, we visited Brezia, a transition home run by a Croatian believer. Brezia provides a place where girls who were too old to live in an orphanage can live for a few months to learn life skills. The girls participate in a micro-enterprise, then "graduate" to independent living. During my visit, the girls who lived there offered me tea. Their caseworker explained that, even one month before, they would not have had the skills or the confidence to serve an outsider. Later, I had the opportunity to visit with a girl whom I'll call Sonja.

Sonja recalled that life in the orphanage had been predictable—everyone was treated the same. There was food, a bed, clothing, and occasional activities. The discipline was harsh, the routine boring.

"Did you ever try to run away?" I asked.

A perplexed look covered her face. "Where would I run to?" was her reply.

"Were you ever afraid?" I asked.

Her greatest fear, she said, was the day when she would have to leave the cold

Social Issues	Possible Responses
Hunger	Soup Kitchens
Inadequate Food	Food Banks
Homelessness	Homeless Shelters
Spouse Abuse	Transition Houses
Neglected Children	Foster Homes
Starving Children	Child Sponsorship
Sexual Assault	Rape Crisis Centers
Human Trafficking	Legislation
Violence and Safety	Neighborhood Watch
Health Care	Trained Workers
Home Care	Meals on Wheels
Care of the Elderly	Nursing Homes
Substance Abuse	Alcoholics Anonymous
Unwanted Pregnancy	Adoption
Crime	Prison Ministries

predictability of the orphanage and begin life on her own—without money, without skills.

Then I asked about Brezia, and she spoke with obvious delight about her life there, where she had learned to tend the garden, prepare meals, clean house, and create beautiful candles for sale. A grin covered her face when I asked how life was different now. "In every way," was the reply.

I asked Sonja a final question. "When you were a child," I wondered, "what were your dreams for the future."

It took Sonja a long time to answer. Finally, she spoke the words I will never forget. She whispered, "I didn't dare to dream."

Like Sonja, many Christians do not dare to dream. We live in a world that is mired with problems. There is poverty, hatred, injustice, and hunger. Faced with what seem to be insurmountable problems, we do not dare to dream of something better.

The world can be a better place. We can change the world through the power of compassion if we have the vision to act.

We Are Paralyzed by Fear

Several years ago, we took a brief holiday in Northern Ireland. One day we planned an excursion to a small island on the northern coast. We loaded our compact car with a large picnic basket and our eager spirits, and we drove until we came to the rugged shoreline. What met us there was a rope bridge, suspended about 250 feet above the roaring ocean and leading to the small island. Until the moment of arrival, I had not considered *how* we were going to get to the island. But now I could see that we were going to walk across an unsteady bridge with only a few wooden slats and a bit of rope between us and the raging sea.

> We can change the world through the power of compassion if we have the vision to act.

Going over, my focus was on the island, the lunch, and on the afternoon with friends. But then the time came to walk back. By then the sun was lower in the sky, casting shadows across our pathway. The sea seemed particularly frothy and noisy, and since the wind had picked up a little, the rope bridge was swaying in both the vertical and horizontal directions.

As our friend placed his foot on the first slat of the bridge, he turned and said in a gentle voice, "Remember, don't look down!"

Now it was my turn.

I took about three steps and then did the forbidden thing—I looked down. Paralyzing terror filled my soul! As I stopped dead in my tracks—three steps out and 250 feet up—I could feel the bridge sway in response to my body weight and the wind. I gripped the rope that served as a railing. I could not move. I could not focus on the land. I could not see our friends who had crossed to the other side. The wind and waves absorbed my complete attention—that and the beating of my heart!

> The prospect of putting love into action can be frightening. Fear robs us of opportunities for showing compassion.

I stood for what seemed like an eternity—probably three or four minutes—and then I heard my husband's voice boom like I have never heard it before. He shouted in an uncharacteristic, military style, "Move!" And I did. One step led to another, and eventually I reached the mainland.

The prospect of putting love into action can be frightening. When we think about reaching out to others, ministering to their needs in the name of Christ, we may become paralyzed with fear, as I was on the bridge. Without doubt, that fear causes errors of omission—we fail to do the good that could be done, show the love that could be shown, and share the hope that we might share. Fear robs us of opportunities for showing compassion.

Yet where there is love to be given, hope to be offered, or where practical acts of kindness are in short supply, there is where Christians *ought* to be. We will never be there if we stand too long on the bridge of fear—fearing the potential ridicule, fearing failure, or self-doubting. Sometimes we need someone to kindly command, *Move!* After the first step, the rest of the journey is easier.

We Are Discouraged by Failure

Recently, I read an essay written by a young woman who learned an important lesson about overcoming failure. At fifteen years of age, she faced a setback that would have discouraged many people. Her positive attitude is a model of the determination we'll need if we are to minister in Jesus' name. Here is what she wrote:

Success: what a feeling!

When I was about nine years old I won my first swimming medal. That began my career as a swimmer. Swimming is my passion and always will be. My parents used to say "From the moment that girl entered the water, we knew she was a swimmer."

Last year I knew that I would have my best chance at winning the provincial championships. As the year passed, inching closer to the championships, I worked hard to set myself up for success.

On the morning of the event, I was pumped up physically, mentally, and emotionally for the competition. Entering the water, energy shot through me like lightning. I was swimming the 400-meter individual medley—four lengths each of backstroke, butterfly, breaststroke, and freestyle—one of the most difficult events, but also my best.

With my heart racing, arms flying, and feet kicking, I powered my way to the finish. Panting for air I looked at the clock—I made it! The year's work had paid off! At five minutes and forty-four seconds, I'd beaten my previous best time by eight seconds. I'd placed second in the province. I shouted with joy as my teammates and coach congratulated me.

Just then, the official motioned for my attention. My heart sank as I thought of the possibilities. Why do they want to talk to me? What did I do?

In a low voice, the woman said, "I'm sorry. You made an illegal turn. You are disqualified from this event."

That failure was disappointing, but I learned something important from the experience. I learned that working hard won't always get you to the top, but it shows the strength of your character. What I wanted to achieve was real, and I had worked hard to achieve it. My attitude towards life changed completely as I realized that the future matters more than the past.

Remember that the future does matter more than the past. You may have attempted to do a great thing for God—and failed. Don't allow that setback to prevent you from showing compassion in the future. Continue to follow the Holy Spirit's leading and you also may come to say, "Success: what a feeling!"

What prevents you from reaching out to meet the needs of others?

A Cup of Cold Water

As Christians, we must translate the love in our hearts into acts of compassion. If we are followers of Jesus Christ, then we must do what He did.

What did Jesus do? He fed the hungry. He washed the disciples' feet. He wept over the death of Lazarus. As we imitate Christ, we will find ourselves feeding, washing, and weeping. Once we have eyes to see the suffering, the desire to do something will grow in our hearts until we put love into action.

Remember, a life of compassion begins with a cup of cold water!

 **To Learn More**

Churches That Make a Difference: Reaching Your Community with Good News and Good Works by Philip N. Olson, Heidi Rolland Unruh, and Ronald J. Sider

Conspiracy of Kindness: A Refreshing New Approach to Sharing the Love of Jesus with Others by Steve Sjogren

Good News and Good Works: A Theology for the Whole Gospel by Ronald J. Sider

Intentional Diversity by Jim Lo

Operation World by Patrick Johnstone and Jason Mandryk

Who's On First edited by Everett Leadingham

All additional books and resources are available from Wesleyan Publishing House at www.wesleyan.org/wph or by calling 800.4.WESLEY (800.493.7539).

Personal Spiritual Journal

DATE _____

_____

_____

_____

_____

_____

_____

_____

_____

_____

_____

_____

_____

_____

_____

_____

My Prayer Today—

_____

_____

_____

_____

CHAPTER 4

The Last Shall Be First

Servant Leadership

> *Whoever wants to become great among you must be your servant.*
>
> —Matthew 20:26

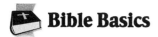 **Bible Basics**

Matthew 20:25–28

²⁵Jesus called them together and said, "You know that the rulers of the Gentiles lord it over them, and their high officials exercise authority over them. ²⁶Not so with you. Instead, whoever wants to become great among you must be your servant, ²⁷and whoever wants to be first must be your slave— ²⁸just as the Son of Man did not come to be served, but to serve, and to give his life as a ransom for many."

Connecting God's Word to Life

In this Scripture, Jesus reveals the essential difference between the world's view of leadership and the Christian's view. What is that key distinction? Name examples of each type of leadership among people you know.

The Heritage of Christian Leadership

Nearly three hundred years ago, a man named John Wesley began a religious movement that spread rapidly across England and North America. We could name several reasons for that. For example, we could point to its theology, emphasizing both the availability of salvation to all and their responsibility to act in faith to receive it. We might also credit the movement's emphasis on personal piety, a devotion so exacting that it was described as "Methodism." Or we might identify the incredible energy of the founder himself, who tirelessly crisscrossed England, preaching to the crowds and shepherding new classes of believers.

But we must not miss another dimension of Wesley's unique genius—this emphasis on leadership development.

At a time when the Church of England limited religious leadership to an educated clergy, Wesley relied on lay leaders and preachers to guide his growing flock of followers. There were other great preachers in Wesley's day, but their influence declined following their deaths. Wesley's well-developed system of leadership, however, supported and strengthened his movement so that his passing in no way inhibited its continued growth. That partnership between pastoral and lay leaders continues to be a key to growth in the church to this day.

In appointing leaders to carry on his work, Wesley was following the pattern for leadership that was modeled by Jesus Himself. Jesus poured His life into leaders that would serve with Him and survive beyond Him. Christ made it clear, though, that He did not mimic the world's pattern of "lording over" others but walked the path of a servant.

Today, you and I must follow in the servant-leader pattern that Christ modeled. Now, you may say that you're not a leader. Oh, but you are! Every one of us influences someone; if in no other way, influence is one way you lead.

What qualities do you think are important in a leader?

Three Dimensional Leadership

Jesus showed His disciples the starting point for leadership. While they were focused on the issue of authority, He told them to adopt the posture of a servant. Being a servant leader begins with being a servant. When a leader has developed a heart to serve God and others, that provides a launch pad for expanding influence into the lives of others.

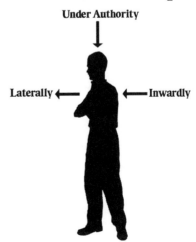

Three Dimensional Servant Leadership

Under Authority

Laterally ← → Inwardly

We live in a self-serve world. From gas pumps to restaurant buffet bars, we choose our options and help ourselves. Some mistakenly label the saying "God helps those who help themselves" as a Bible verse. It's really a reflection of the North American can-do spirit. Servant leadership requires serving God and others in a self-serving world. Before a person can be effective in leading others, he or she must develop servant leadership in three ways.

Self-Leadership: Leading Inwardly

The first requirement for a servant leader is to lead oneself. That requires the discipline to consistently submit myself to God's will and focus on the best interests of others. The Apostle Paul describes self-leadership this way in Phil. 2:3–7:

> ³Do nothing out of selfish ambition or vain conceit, but in humility consider others better than yourselves. ⁴Each of you should look not only to your own interests, but also to the interests of others. ⁵Your attitude should be the same as that of Christ Jesus: ⁶Who, being in very nature God, did not consider equality with God something to be grasped, ⁷but made himself nothing, taking the very nature of a servant, being made in human likeness.

This passage does not negate the validity of godly ambition or having our own interests. Rather it disciplines and elevates those ambitions and interests for greater service to God and others.

God has ingrained this lesson into my character at various defining moments in my life. One of those moments came during my senior year of college. Through a prayer partnership with a good friend, God laid a burden for church planting upon my heart and called me to plant a church in a specific area of a particular city. That God-given vision clarified some of the dreams I had for making a difference in ministry. But that vision was also diluted by my personal pride and concern for selfish interests.

I had envisioned myself as the founding pastor of a new congregation. At twenty-one years of age, I wanted the recognition that being the leader in this enterprise might bring. God, in His grace, allowed me to be in on the ground floor of a brand new work, but not as the founding pastor. That role was filled on a part-time basis by the respected leader of a parachurch ministry in the area. I was offered the position of assistant pastor on a full-time basis, submitting to the senior pastor's direction.

> The first requirement for a servant leader is to lead oneself.

In retrospect, I believe that God was checking my heart to see if my interest in the church had more to do with serving or leading. He was pushing me to uncover the real motive—was my involvement in this new church driven by the hunger for position or the passion to serve? I'm embarrassed to admit that I wrestled with God far too long before joining this wonderful endeavor as assistant pastor.

During my two years as assistant pastor, the senior pastor served and mentored me in a tremendous way. I wouldn't trade that experience for anything. Then, when he moved to Chicago, I was offered the position of senior pastor. By that time God has rooted out some of my arrogance, and I was humbled to step into the leader's role. And I was grateful that there was now more "servant" in my leadership.

Many secular studies of leadership have discovered the principle that Jesus taught from the beginning—leadership begins with internal attitudes, the taming of self. Daniel Goleman, in his ground breaking work on emotional intelligence,[1] says that a person's success in life begins with self-awareness. By that he means the

> ## Leadership begins with internal attitudes, the taming of self.

capacity to accurately assess one's strengths and weaknesses. For a Christian, this self-awareness is the foundation of service. As the Apostle Paul put it, "For by the grace given me I say to every one of you: Do not think of yourself more highly than you ought, but rather think of yourself with sober judgment, in accordance with the measure of faith God has given you" (Rom. 12:3). A Christian's self-awareness is characterized by both sober judgment and a measure of faith. Without sober judgment, visions of grandeur set us up for a fall. Without a measure of faith, our leadership potential is limited to our human ability, discounting the power of God.

Goleman goes on to say that the second characteristic of emotional intelligence is self-discipline. By that he means the capacity to form good habits and correct bad ones. As Christians, we have the edge in that area, "for God did not give us a spirit of timidity, but a spirit of power, of love and of self-discipline" (2 Tim. 1:7). For us, self-discipline is a byproduct of God's Spirit living within us. That results in, among other things, self-control (Gal. 5:23). Goleman says that self-awareness and self-discipline are the foundation of all other characteristics of effective people. They are marks of self-leadership.

In his book *Good to Great*, Jim Collins describes the key quality found in leaders of the most successful companies in America. He labels this key trait "Level Five Leadership," and describing those who possess it as building "enduring greatness through a paradoxical blend of personal humility and professional will."[2]

That statement applies to all biblical leaders who finished well!

These are biblical components of a biblical style of leadership that honors God. The Bible makes it clear that personal humility is not only recommended but is required for servant leaders. God opposes the proud, but gives grace to the humble

(1 Pet. 5:5–6). And Collins's idea of professional will correspond to the biblical quality of perseverance (James 1:2–4). Humility and perseverance are repeatedly exhibited in the lives of people God has used throughout history.

What are some strengths that God has placed in your life that you wish to develop more fully? What are some weaknesses in your life that you wish to discipline more consistently?

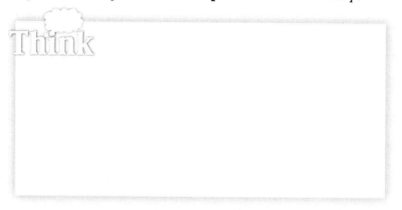

"Followership": Leading under Authority

A servant leader must be able to work under the authority of someone else. One of the people who impressed Jesus the most was someone who understood both how to exercise authority and how to work under it (see Luke 7:1–10). This man, a Roman centurion, exhibited a level of faith that amazed Jesus and prompted Him to grant the centurion's request.

Following Christ. It's impossible to be a good leader without learning to be a good follower. Paul understood that when he confidently invited others to "follow my example as I follow the example of Christ" (1 Cor. 11:1). To be a servant leader implies that there is a master, and that master is the Head of the Church, Jesus Christ. To the extent that every corner of our lives is fully surrendered to Him, His power can operate fully in us.

The story of Nebuchadnezzar (Dan. 4) is an excellent reminder of this principle. Nebuchadnezzar was a king who began to believe that he was the ultimate ruler of the ultimate kingdom. This perception of himself at the top of the organizational chart prompted a dramatic warning from God followed by tragic consequences. Nebuchadnezzar, who had once ruled the greatest kingdom of his day, lost his mind and found himself grazing in the fields like an animal. Then, when God restored his sanity, Nebuchadnezzar readily acknowledged that any authority he exercised had been given to him by God.

The God who delegates His authority can easily remove that authority from those who fail to follow Him.

As a pastor, my capacity to lead a congregation depends on my receptivity to the leading of the Holy Spirit. If I stop seeking the Holy Spirit's direction or fail to follow it readily, God may send me out to "graze in the fields," removing his blessing from my ministry.

> For the servant leader, "following the leader" is not child's play. It is the essence of effectiveness.

I am not the owner of my leadership position. I am a steward of the power that God chooses to exercise through me. I am the servant; He is the Master. *The Living Bible* paraphrase of 1 Chron. 29:11b–12 reinforces this reality:

> [11]Everything in the heavens and earth is yours, O LORD, and this is your kingdom. We adore you as being in control of everything. [12]Riches and honor come from you alone, and you are the Ruler of all mankind. Your hand controls power and might, and it is at your discretion that men are made great and given strength.

For the servant leader, "following the leader" is not child's play. It is the essence of effectiveness. We must become the servant of One before we can become the servant of all.

Following Others. It's one thing to follow God directly. In a sense, that requires little humility. He is so great and we are so small that there's simply no comparison. But what about following others to whom God has delegated His authority? They are flawed individuals, and we may have areas of strength in the very areas where they are weak.

Watchman Nee, in his classic book *Spiritual Authority*,[3] explores this issue extensively. Nee rightly concludes that our capacity to be used by God is increased not only by following God directly but also by following others whom God has placed in authority. The author of Hebrews commands us to "obey your leaders and submit to their authority" (13:17). Many people aspire to leadership because they are restless, if not rebellious, under the authority of others. God may well place us under the authority of another person so that we may learn to serve, and by doing so become servant leaders.

On a scale of 1 to 10, how responsive are you to the leading of the Holy Spirit in your life? To the leadership of others? What can do to improve your ability to listen and follow?

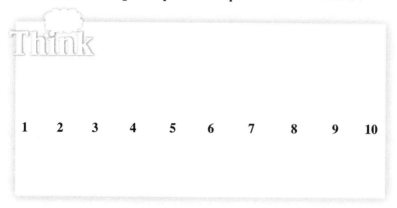

Think

1   2   3   4   5   6   7   8   9   10

Partnership: Leading Laterally

Becoming a servant leader requires self-leadership, "followership," and one more crucial ingredient: partnership. Partnership is how we relate to our peers. It is our capacity to form strategic relationships and work as a team with those who serve along side us.

As members of the body of Christ, we belong to each other (Rom. 12:4–8). We can respond fully to the Head, Jesus Christ, only as we cooperate other parts of the body. If we treat either others or ourselves as unnecessary, the body is handicapped (1 Cor. 12:12–26). When we properly value and manage the gifts God has given to others and to us, we work as a team. In this way, the many gifts that God has placed in His Church may be fully exercised. We are partners in the gospel enterprise.

> God may well place us under the authority of another person so that we may learn to serve, and by doing so become servant leaders.

Leading laterally means developing our ability to influence and serve those who work with us. That happens as we develop relationships that build trust by constructive cooperation rather than destructive competition.

The church where I serve is led by a rather large staff. Some years ago we neglected the partnership aspect of servant leadership. As a result, we experienced what might be called the *silo effect*. While each of us was effective in his or her various area of responsibility, there was little awareness of or appreciation for what others were doing. We existed in silos, self-contained worlds that began and ended with our ministry responsibilities. This resulted in poorly orchestrated efforts in pursuing our common mission.

So we began to create opportunities to celebrate what was happening in each other's area of ministry. We found little ways to serve and support each other. We became intentional about praying for each other and sending notes of encouragement. This slowly lowered the walls of our silos and increased the effectiveness of our overall ministry. It also enlarged our hearts as servant leaders.

Are you currently supporting your peers in faith? What one thing could you do to let your peers know that you support their work?

Priorities for Leading Others

As we become three-dimensional leaders—aligned with God, ourselves, and our peers—we are positioned to become servant leaders of others. In becoming a leader, there are two equally dangerous extremes that can cause imbalance.

Avoiding the Extremes

One extreme is using others. This utilitarian approach to leadership views people as the warm bodies necessary to fill holes in an organizational chart. The focus is on the leader and his or her goals. This extreme is self-serving rather than truly loving. It has a dehumanizing effect on others. Selfish leadership is evidenced by:

- Being interested in others only if they can contribute to the goal.
- Talking about the task to be accomplished without listening to the personal concerns of those involved.
- Ignoring others once they've been enlisted, always turning attention to the next "recruit."

While this approach may exhibit strong starting power, it rarely results in the staying power necessary to accomplish something for the glory of God. One of the rich payoffs in serving with others is the experience of community. As servant leaders we create a context for relationships where those serving together also share together.

The other dangerous extreme for a leader is pleasing others. This issue is more complex because there are legitimate benefits from pleasing others. The Apostle Paul expresses a desire to "please everybody in every way" in order that they might be saved (1 Cor. 10:33). But he also says, "If I were still trying to please men, I would not be a servant of Christ" (Gal. 1:10). On another occasion he states, "We are not trying to please men but God, who tests our hearts" (1 Thess. 2:4).

> One of the rich payoffs for serving with others is the experience of community.

What's the difference? In the first case, pleasing others builds bridges for communicating the gospel and the developing of spiritual maturity. In the latter cases, pleasing people would result in outcomes displeasing to God. The extreme of people pleasing is evidenced by:

- Feeling good about something only when everyone else feels good about it.
- Acting only based on consensus rather than conviction.
- Telling people what they want to hear rather than what they need to hear.

In the words of John Maxwell, "I can give you a formula for failure—try to please everyone."

Orville Butcher, a retired minister of great influence, once said, "The problem with most churches is not who we're willing to reach, but who we're unwilling to lose." He wasn't sanctioning insensitivity. He was recognizing that many leaders are held captive to the whims of a small minority of the people they lead. This compulsion to please everyone can take the edge off our faith and produces a mediocrity that will be palatable, but not fruitful.

The balanced approach to servant leadership involves loving and leading others while avoiding the extremes of people using and people pleasing. That balanced approach is conducted in several ways.

Mark your leadership style below. Do you tend toward the extreme of using others or pleasing others? What can you do to bring balance in this area of your life?

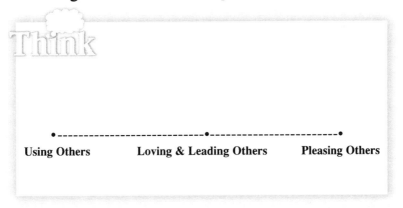

•--------------------------------•------------------------•

Using Others   **Loving & Leading Others**   **Pleasing Others**

Coaching

An effective leader will coach others to hear God's call upon their lives. That involves prayerfully identifying individuals in whom to invest time, then coaching them to develop two core capacities.

The Capacity to Sense and Obey God's Leading. This challenge calls people to clarify their servant profile—their ministry passions, spiritual gifts, and personal style. The goal is to create a statement that captures their calling (life purpose) and identifying some low cost ways to begin moving in that direction.

The Capacity to Shape and Invest in a Ministry with Kingdom Impact. This challenge begins with clearly understanding the mission and vision of your local church. You'll want to learn about the various ministry opportunities. That's important because discipleship involves learning by participation. You will develop as you experiment in various ministries with meaningful feedback from the leader.

The saying goes that "experience is a great teacher." In fact, many people have lots of experiences and still learn nothing! It would be more accurate to say that evaluated experience is a great teacher. A servant leader provides a safe place where followers can reflect upon their service and glean insight from it.

This coaching can be done either one-to-one, in a class, or in small groups. Without it, many people will not translate the vague notion that God may have some work for them to do into a concrete plan of action. They need the insight and support that is best provided in personal or group settings.

Love

A second priority for a servant leader is to love others. That is, to love others enough to address their true needs, not just their felt needs. We must "speak the truth in love" to prompt others to seek holiness and to commit themselves fully to God.

While love is often expressed with emotion, it is primarily an action. Loving action is always done in the best interest of another person. Because we are primarily servants of Christ, we act to bring about His purpose for those we lead. As we pray for them, God may well give us insight into their deepest needs. We must

> Loving action is always done in the best interest of another person.

share these revelations with generous amounts of affirmation but also with the expectation that, by God's grace, people will change and grow as disciples of Christ.

Assimilation

An effective leader will also assimilate others into a God-honoring movement—one that is mission driven not personality dependent. The more personality centered an organization is, the less mission driven it will be.

Since I have been privileged to serve as a pastor of my current congregation from its inception, there are some natural ways in the church is a reflection of me. Those who relate well to me tend to stay here, and those who don't often leave! Many people look to me for guidance in making decisions, and others connect with my approach to teaching. Those dynamics apply to most leadership situations.

While that is useful, it can be easily overdone. One reason many long-term leaders leave such a void when they depart is that the organization is overly dependent upon their personality and energy. The mission suffers as a result.

As a servant leaders, we must determine that our ministries will become fully functional in pursuing their mission and vision without being dependent upon any one person. Over time, that will place the focus more on the mission than on any individual. Servant leaders create disciples, not dependents.

Impact

A fourth area of concern for a leader of others is impact. Servant leaders impact others with their God-given gifts. Our Master, the Head of the Body, Jesus Christ, has given us gifts to invest into the lives of others. Servant leaders have both a major and a minor when it comes to ministry emphasis.

We major in the areas where God has gifted us. The majority of our time and our investment in the lives of others should make use of our primary spiritual gifts. For example, a person whose primary gifts are leadership and prophecy should arrange his or her time in order to maximize the use of those abilities.

Leaders should minor in areas where they can offer simple acts of service and random acts of kindness. Occasionally I serve in the nursery, help with the church landscaping, and set up chairs for events. I don't have the gifts of mercy or helps, but I am part of a local church body that needs me to serve in those ways periodically. These commitments do not fill large blocks of time, but I want to be sure I'm participating in them with some of my time.

God wouldn't give me certain gifts and then call me to exercise the majority of my ministry in an area that never makes use of them. Neither must I hide behind the excuse "that's not my gift" when occasional acts of service are required.

Of the four dimensions of loving and leading others—coaching, love, assimilation, and impact—which area needs your attention right now?

Accountability

People cringe at the very mention of the word *accountability*. In a society that emphasizes freedom and privacy, accountability seems to threaten our basic rights. As Christians, we talk about it much but practice it little. Yet as servant leaders, we belong to the kingdom of God and live to fulfill an eternal purpose. We live in community, not privacy. We are free but are commanded to use that freedom to serve (Gal. 5:13). Accountability is not optional for a servant leader. We are accountable both to God and to others in several ways.

Vertical Accountability

Ultimately, we are accountable to God. "So then, each of us will give an account of himself to God" (Rom. 14:12). Our salvation, made possible by the grace of God alone, frees us from eternal judgment. Our stewardship, what we accomplish through faithful use of the time, talent, and treasure entrusted to us, will result in an eternal assessment.

Jesus often communicated spiritual principles through stories. On one occasion He compared the kingdom of heaven to a man who went on a journey and entrusted the management of his money to servants (Matt. 25:14–30). The amount entrusted to each of them was related to their ability. When the master returned, they were called in to settle accounts. Those who were faithful in the management of their master's property produced a good income and were rewarded. But one of the servants questioned his master's character and was lazy. He did nothing to improve on the sum entrusted to him. His unfaithfulness resulted in the master's judgment.

> As servants, we have different abilities and responsibilities. Yet we all must be faithful and fruitful.

As servants, we have different abilities and responsibilities. God decides what we will receive. Yet we all must be faithful and fruitful. Each of us will give an account to God, the Master. So we study God's Word to know what He expects and then diligently fulfill those expectations until His return.

The present tendency among Christians is to celebrate God's grace, and rightfully so. Our salvation is not the result of our own hard work. But this nearly exclusive focus on grace has led us to neglect the good work that God expects us to be doing. One of the Scriptures that states most clearly that we are saved by grace goes on to say that those who have experienced salvation now have work to do! (Eph. 2:8–10). We will not stand before God alongside those who are destined for eternal separation from Him, but "we must all appear before the judgment seat of Christ, that each one may receive what is due him for the things done while in the body, whether good or bad" (2 Cor. 5:10). The gracious God we serve will hold us accountable.

Horizontal Accountability

The writer of Ecclesiastes observed long ago the power of two or more people who are joined in a meaningful relationship:

> [9]Two are better than one, because they have a good return for their work: [10]If one falls down, the other can help him up. But pity the man who falls and

has no one to help him up! ¹¹Also, if two lie down together, they will keep warm. But how can one keep warm alone? ¹²Though one may be overpowered, two can defend themselves. A cord of three strands is not quickly broken (Eccles. 4:9–12).

By uniting with others, we are both more productive and more protected.

John Wesley built accountability into his weekly gatherings of believers. They would regularly confess areas of sin and report on areas of temptation. Wesley knew that holy living and passionate service could not be completely cultivated in isolation.

Accountability Partners. One way a leader can create horizontal accountability is to establish an accountability partner.

The format for accountability partnering is simple. Choose a partner, someone whom you trust to share some details of your "private world," then establish a time to meet together, review accountability goals, and pray for one another. Accountability goals covers all

> Wesley knew that holy living and passionate service could not be cultivated in isolation.

life areas and contain questions that can be answered either "Yes, I have" or "No, I haven't." For example:

Life Area—Spiritual

_____ I have read the Bible daily on a pace to complete it in one year.

_____ I have prayed daily for at least twenty minutes.

_____ I have memorized a Scripture verse in the last month.

_____ I have fasted at least one meal in the last month.

Life Area—Physical

_____ I have maintained a weight under my goal weight.

_____ I have exercised at least thirty minutes at least three times a week.

_____ I have slept an average of seven to eight hours each night.

Other life areas include relational (marriage, family, friendships), vocational (career, finances), and personal (ways to grow mentally, emotionally, volitionally). It's best to begin with about ten goals, although you will likely add more. It may also be best to select areas where you have had some success but where greater consistency is needed.

Leadership Accountability. Leadership accountability focuses on a leader's responsibilities. One way of creating leadership accountability is to create a Ministry Action Plan (MAP). The MAP details the areas where the leader and his or her supervisor agree to focus effort for the coming year.

On a quarterly basis, the leader reports to progress in achieving the MAP to his or her supervisor. On many occasions, issues may surface that would otherwise have simmered beneath the surface. This process may also reveal blind spots that could be proactively addressed before they result in negative consequences.

A wise leader will also seek 360-degree feedback. This is feedback from those who serve along side and under the leader. The servant leader must receive this input openly and non-defensively. That isn't always easy, but the feedback is so valuable for self-development that you won't want to risk going without it.

Who provides accountability in your life? What could you do to strengthen these accountability relationships or add others?

The process of growing as a servant leader is life long. In the words of Robert Schuller, "the danger is not in striving, but arriving." Robert Clinton, who has committed his life to the study of leadership, estimates that "70 percent of Christian leaders don't finish well." By "finishing well," Clinton means more than merely avoiding moral failure. He means remaining teachable, paying attention to character issues, being intimate with Christ, and leaving behind contributions of eternal worth.

Servant leaders don't focus only on the starting line—they focus on the finish line. They are marathoners for the Master.

To Learn More

Accountability: Becoming People of Integrity by Yvonne Prowant and Wayne Schmidt.

Follow the Leader: A Daily Spiritual Journey by Norman G. Wilson

Leading from the Inside Out: The Art of Self-Leadership by Samuel D. Rima

People Just Like Us by Norman G. Wilson

Success! edited by Everett Leadingham

All additional books and resources are available from Wesleyan Publishing House at www.wesleyan.org/wph or by calling 800.4.WESLEY (800.493.7539).

Personal Spiritual Journal

DATE _____

_____

_____

_____

_____

_____

_____

_____

_____

_____

_____

_____

_____

_____

My Prayer Today—

_____

_____

_____

_____

CHAPTER 5

God's Plan from the Beginning

Family

> *And live a life of love, just as Christ loved us and gave*
> *himself up for us as a fragrant offering and sacrifice to God.*
> —Ephesians 5:2

 **Bible Basics**

Genesis 1:27–28

[27]So God created man in his own image, in the image of God he created him; male and female he created them. [28]God blessed them and said to them, "Be fruitful and increase in number; fill the earth and subdue it. Rule over the fish of the sea and the birds of the air and over every living creature that moves on the ground."

Ephesians 4:32–5:3

[32]Be kind and compassionate to one another, forgiving each other, just as in Christ God forgave you. [1]Be imitators of God, therefore, as dearly loved children [2]and live a life of love, just as Christ loved us and gave himself up for us as a fragrant offering and sacrifice to God. [3]But among you there must not be even a hint of sexual immorality, or of any kind of impurity, or of greed, because these are improper for God's holy people.

 Connecting God's Word to Life

From these Scriptures, list several key words that describe an ideal family life. What values do you consider important for a family?

Family Is God's Idea

The family is as old as Adam and Eve. God created the family in the Garden of Eden. It is His way of saying, "This is the best way for you to live." Family is the basic unit of society and the guarantee of our future.

It all began with Adam. God created a beautiful world for Adam to live in. It overflowed with delicious fruits, colorful flowers, and a variety of animals. And Adam had work to do—tending the garden and naming the animals. Who wouldn't be happy in that paradise? Yet even the Garden of Eden was not enough for Adam. He was lonely for human companionship.

God observed Adam and remarked, "It is not good for the man to be alone. I will make a helper suitable for him" (Gen. 2:18). Then He created Eve to be a wife for Adam, and the first family began.

The Purpose of Family

When God created Adam and Eve, He established some essential truths about family life. This first family, one man and one woman, was created to tend the garden together and to bear children (Gen. 1:26, 28). Their partnership was not simply for their own fulfillment. It had a purpose.

Also, God wanted to relate to this couple. They were created for fellowship with their Creator. God stipulated that those who would enter into marriage would "leave their father and mother" and become attached to their spouses (Gen. 2:24).

God's Purpose for Marriage	
In the Garden of Eden	**Today**
To rule over creation and tend the garden (Gen. 1:26; 2:15)	To support and help one another
To multiply (Gen. 1:28)	To bear and raise children
To have fellowship with God (Gen. 3:8–9)	To worship God as a family

The Gift of Gender

Who is more like God—your mother or your father? If you look beyond the moral character of each person, you may observe that men and women, by their nature, are like God in certain ways. For example, we tend to associate masculine characteristics such as strength and dominance with God. But an equal number of godlike characteristics are usually considered feminine, such as tenderness, nurturing, and empathy.

That gives new meaning in the words, "So God created man in his own image, in the image of God he created him; male and female he created them" (Gen. 1:27). Somehow, the image of God is more fully reflected in Adam and Eve together than in either one of them alone. Both genders have value, so a married couple jointly reflects the image of God in the fullest way possible. (That also implies that same-sex union is clearly not God's plan.)

Equality of the Sexes

The New Testament adds to our understanding of God's plan for marriage. While men and women may serve different roles in the family, Scripture insists that we look beyond gender differences to affirm that men and women are completely equal before God. Paul writes, "There is neither Jew nor Greek, slave nor free, male nor female, for you are all one in Christ Jesus" (Gal. 3:28). Peter urged husbands to understand that their

> Scripture affirms that men and women are equal before God.

wives are "heirs with you of the gracious gift of life" (1 Pet. 3:7). After all, Jesus had already taught that in heaven people will not be married, for current sexual roles will be transcended (Matt. 22:30).

God's Blessing on Marriage

After God created Adam and Eve as the first family, He blessed them and pronounced that all He had made was "very good" (Gen. 1:28, 31). Marriage and the family have God's explicit blessing and approval.

All of us, regardless of marital status, are part of families, and we can model the characteristics of a godly home. Let's learn more about those and what we can do to develop strong marriages and families.

Why do you think God created marriage?

Honoring the Marriage Covenant

A covenant is a solemn agreement by both parties, usually sealed by a ritual and having an accompanying sign. For example, after the flood, God promised that there would never again be a universal flood. The covenant was sealed by a sacrifice and the sign of the rainbow was given (Gen. 9:8–16). God also made a covenant with Abraham that had an accompanying sign (Gen. 15:8–21, 17:10). Perhaps the best example of a covenant is God's agreement with the Israelites at Mount Sinai. Israel agreed to keep God's laws, and God agreed to bless and protect them.

Marriage is a covenant. It is an agreement between one man and one woman, made before God, in which they pledge exclusive devotion to one another for life. The covenant is sealed by a ritual—the wedding ceremony. The accompanying sign for marriage is not the wedding ring, but sexual intercourse. The Bible says that a man will "be united to his wife, and they will become one flesh" (Gen. 2:24). God created the sexual act to be the covenant sign. It is the culmination of the bonding process between husband and wife and is a continuing force in maintaining the marital bond.

Biblical Covenants				
Covenant	Those Involved	Ritual	Sign	Agreement
Noahic Covenant	God and Noah	Sacrifice at Ararat	Rainbow	God will not Destroy the Earth by Flood
Abrahamic Covenant	God and Abraham	Smoking Pot and Torch Passed between Halves of Sacrificed Animals	Circumcision	God Promised to Give the Canaan to Abraham's Descendants
Mosaic Covenant	God and the Nation Israel	Events at Mt. Sinai	Sabbath Observance	Israel Would Obey Ten Commandments God Would Bless Israel
The Marriage Covenant	A Husband and a Wife	The Wedding	Sexual Intercourse	Both Pledge Love and Faithfulness for Life

The Importance of Fidelity

Covenants must be honored. The Bible repeatedly shows that God is faithful in keeping His covenants. God's faithfulness is often contrasted with Israel's unfaithfulness, which the Bible compares to adultery. The life of the prophet Hosea is a powerful illustration of the value of faithfulness. God commanded Hosea to marry a promiscuous woman as an illustration of Israel's unfaithfulness to God (Hos. 1:2). When Hosea's wife deserted him, God told him to bring her back, even though she was working as a prostitute (Hos. 3:1–2). Hosea's unwavering love for her was a poignant illustration of God's faithfulness to His covenant obligations. He is faithful, even when we are not.

As believers, it's important that we honor our marriage covenants. God intends for us to be faithful to our marriage partners.

Two of the Ten Commandments reinforce the importance of faithfulness in marriage: the seventh, "You shall not commit adultery," and a portion of the tenth, "You shall not covet your neighbor's wife" (Exod. 20:14, 17). Jesus also strongly affirmed the sanctity of marriage when He cited the Genesis model for marriage and said, "Therefore what God has joined together, let man not separate" (Matt. 19:6). In fact, Jesus wanted to protect marriage so strongly that He declared the sin of lust to be equivalent to adultery (Matt. 5:28). This elevation of marriage reached a new level when Paul explained that the relationship of a husband and a wife is a model of the spiritual relationship between Christ and His church (Eph. 5:21, 25, 26, 32).

Threats to Fidelity

God wants us to honor our marriage covenants. Most people want that too. Yet unfaithfulness is all too common, even among believers. Many factors threaten marriage and undermine our ability to remain faithful.

Pre-marital Sex. Sex before marriage, which the Bible labels "sexual immorality," is clearly prohibited by Scripture (1 Cor. 10:8, Gal. 5:19, Eph. 5:3, 1 Thess. 4:3). Yet today, many people limit the definition of sexual immorality to include only casual or promiscuous sex, or adultery. Many people do not think of cohabitation or a "committed relationship" as wrong. But the Bible clearly indicates that all sexual relationships outside marriage are harmful. For example, in the Law of Moses, if a man had sex with a "virgin who [was] not pledged to be married," he had to marry her (Deut. 22:28–29).

> God wants us to honor our marriage covenants. Most people want that too.

Christ wants the Church, His bride, to be "without stain or wrinkle . . . holy and blameless" (Eph. 5:27). This description mirrors a good spouse's desire for a partner who has not been united with another. To preserve that purity, sex must be reserved for marriage.

As Josh McDowell has pointed out, "God gave us commands . . . because he wanted to protect and provide for us."[1] In limiting sex to marriage, God aimed to protect the bond between the partners and provide the greatest sexual happiness of the marital couple. Chastity protects us from guilt, unplanned pregnancy, and sexually transmitted diseases. It provides a strong foundation of trust and a more secure relationship in which to raise children. As masking tape sticks less each time it is reapplied to a surface, so the capacity for human sexual bonding is weakened by a succession of sexual partners. Our culture's high premium on "so-called social experience is contributing to patterns of promiscuity and its defective bonding,"[2] while God's plan for chastity provides for maximum strength pair bonding.

This truth is supported by research. In a University of Wisconsin study, 27 percent of those who lived together before marriage reported distress in their relationship after thirty months while only 13 percent of those who did not live together reported distress. In addition, 38 percent of the couples who lived together before marriage were divorced within ten years. For those who had not cohabited, the divorce rate was 27 percent.[3]

Benefits of Chastity before Marriage[4]	
Protects From	Provides For
Guilt	Spiritual rewards
Unplanned pregnancy	Optimum atmosphere for child rearing
Sexually transmitted diseases	Peace of mind
Sexual insecurity	Trust
Emotional distress	True intimacy
Weakened sexual bonding	Maximum strength sexual bonding

Cultural Influence. The skewed portrayal of human sexuality by the media is another force that undermines marital fidelity. Sexual innuendo fills primetime television and even sneaks into some cartoons. Movies include increasingly graphic sexual content. Pornography is more available today than ever.

Jesus taught that thoughts are the seeds of action. He said, "Out of the heart come evil thoughts, murder, adultery, sexual immorality" (Matt. 15:19). He also made clear that sexual sin can be committed with the mind alone: "I tell you that anyone who looks at a woman lustfully has already committed adultery with her in his heart" (Matt. 5:28).

To remain faithful in marriage, we must carefully consider which words and images we allow to enter our minds through the media. We should restrict our exposure to media content that dulls our sensitivity to the horror of sexual sin, or—even worse—tempts us to sin. It is impossible to enjoy immoral behavior vicariously and maintain the highest standard of sexual fidelity.

What poses the greatest threat to your sexual fidelity? What will you do to eliminate that risk?

Creating an Atmosphere of Love

Many children's stories conclude with the familiar words "and they lived happily ever after." Anyone who has been married will tell you that that's not as easy as it sounds! After the thrilling experience of the wedding, a married couple must establish a home. Two people must learn to live together in harmony. How is that done? There are at least five elements of a loving home.

Love

God is love, and a Christian home should reflect God's love. Yet since our culture uses the word *love* to describe everything from a casual affinity ("I love spaghetti") to sexual intercourse ("I make love to my wife"), it is important to define what love really means.

The Apostle John explains, "This is how we know what love is: Jesus Christ laid down his life for us. And we ought to lay down our lives for our brothers" (1 John 3:16). Paul makes that even more specific. "Husbands, love your wives, just as Christ loved the church and gave himself up for her" (Eph. 5:25).

Love is a self-giving affection that puts the needs of another person above our own. This kind of love does not ask, "What's in this for me?" Rather, it asks, "What does my loved one need?"

When Greg attended his wife's high school reunion, he received a high compliment. Recognizing how his wife had grown as a person since graduation, one of her classmates said to Greg, "You must be good for her." That's the aim of Christian love—to do good for another.

> Love is a self-giving affection that puts the needs of another person above our own.

"A marriage relationship can unfold like a stunning rose blossom when each person has built his or her own personal identity and security upon an understanding of God's love," writes H. Norman Wright. "Each learns to derive values from God, rather than from performance, status, or appearance."[5]

Respect

Respect is a second element of a godly home. Here's how the Bible defines the respect that married people should give to each other. The Apostle Paul wrote, "Each one of you also must love his wife as he loves himself, and the wife must respect her husband" (Eph. 5:33). The Apostle Peter added, "Husbands, in the same way be considerate as you live with your wives, and treat them with respect" (1 Pet. 3:7). Josh McDowell summed it up this way: "Respectful treatment of others creates a solid foundation for relationships."[22]

One way many couples show disrespect for each other is through their speech. Name-calling and negative labeling all too easily slip into our communication, especially when we're angry. We must be on guard against that. Public putdowns, even in jest, and condescending speech are disrespectful too

In place of such selfish speech, loving couples build one another up with words of appreciation, affirmation, and encouragement (1 Thess. 5:11; Eph. 4:29).

List some ways you can show respect for your spouse.

Responsibility

In a godly family, partners share responsibility and work together to make the family function. That was true in the Garden of Eden, and is today. The command to "carry each other's burdens" (Gal. 6:2) applies to marriage as well as to other relationships.

Mutual Submission

North American culture teaches the value of independence. That fits well with our natural desire to want things our own way. In a marriage, however, that attitude may lead two people to live separate lives in the same house.

In stark contrast to the prevailing "me first" attitude of our day, the Bible commands couples to "submit to one another out of reverence for Christ" (Eph. 5:21). Often, the word *submit* brings to mind the image of authority. We picture one partner completely dominating the other. That's not what the Bible teaches. In fact, both of the Scriptures that refer to this subject speak to both husbands and wives (Eph. 5:21–33; 1 Pet. 3:1–12).

Paul best defines the idea of submission: "Husbands, love your wives, just as

Christ loved the church and gave himself up for her" (Eph. 5:25). Submitting to one's partner means to consider his or her needs above your own. Steve and Annie Chapman write, "Lasting romance begins when a husband and wife start viewing marriage as a chance to meet each other's needs."[7] While the Bible assigns leadership at home to the husband, the concept of mutual submission demands that he be a sacrificial servant leader, as Christ was.

Permanence

God planned for marriage to be a lifelong union. While Scripture recognizes that divorce is sometimes permissible because of our sin, divorce is not part of God's original plan (Matt. 19:3–12; Mal. 2:10, 16). The permanence of Christian marriages reflects the unchangeable love of God for His people. Divorce, on the other hand, breaks the vow to love "till death do us part."

Like all of God's commands, the command that marriage should be permanent is intended to protect and provide for us. The stability of the marriage is the rock upon which the emotional security of the whole family rests. Everyone thrives in a home that has an atmosphere of permanence.

Permanence—
the Foundation of a Secure Home

Raising Godly Children

When God sent His Son into this world as a baby, He chose a human family to instruct, nurture, and be a model for His own Son (Luke 2:51–52). That reinforces the biblical teaching that God ordained the family as the institution to provide for and train children. That shaping process takes place in a number of ways.

Loving

The love of a parent teaches children about the love of God. We learn about His unconditional love when our parents love us in spite of our childlike shortcomings (1 Cor. 13:4–7). We first understand that love is self-sacrificing when we see Mom and Dad putting our needs ahead of their own. From infancy, we learn that love speaks gently as we hear the affectionate words of our parents. A loving home produces loving children.

Actions as well as words must be used to demonstrate love. There are five specific actions that cause people to feel loved: physical touch, quality time, gifts, acts of service, and words of affirmation.[8] Jesus spoke all five love languages in His ministry to people. As our lives show love all five concrete ways, our homes become sanctuaries of love.

Five Languages of Love		
Love Language	Name an Occasion When Jesus Used This Language	Name One Way You Can Speak This Language at Home
Words of Affirmation		
Physical Touch		
Quality Time		
Gifts		
Acts of Service		

Training

In order to train their children, parents must establish their authority. Love is the foundation for that authority. Discipline can only be successful when a child knows that he or she is loved.

The Bible says, "Fools despise wisdom and discipline" (Prov. 1:7b). Children must be taught the meaning of the word *no* from a young age. The Bible says that parents who truly love their children are "careful to discipline" them (Prov. 13:24). When the children grow up in a home with effective discipline, they learn to discipline themselves.

When the foundation of love and authority has been laid, effective training is possible. Scripture admonishes parents to bring their children up "in the training and instruction of the Lord" (Eph. 6:4). That task encompasses all of our daily lives. God says, "These commandments that I give you today are to be upon your hearts. Impress them on your children. Talk about them when you sit at home and when you walk along the road, when you lie down and when you get up" (Deut. 6:6–7). Teachable moments can happen in the kitchen, while riding in the car, or while doing daily chores.

Training children also includes instruction in the faith. Loving parents teach their children Bible truth and bring them to church, Sunday School, and other healthy learning environments.

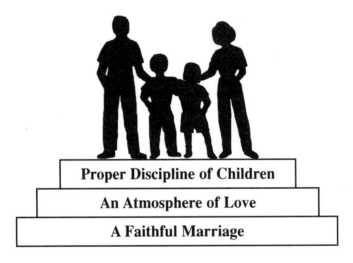

Building Blocks of a Godly Home

Modeling Relationships

Children always copy what they see. Just watch a little girl playing house, and you'll be sure to hear her mother's words echoed back. Children first learn how to interact with other people by watching Mom and Dad.

That's why it's important for parents to model good relationships, attitudes, and behaviors in their homes. Children store away parenting and marriage skills that they see in their parents and use them later in life. As we model godly traits such as respectful speech, self-control, expressing our needs acceptably, and handling anger well, we lay the foundation for our children's future success in their relationships.

Children discover the importance of our beliefs by watching the way we live. If we say that worship is important but seldom attend church, our children will learn that faith is of little value. Our children watch our lives closely.

Children will learn to pray as parents pray with them at bedtime, mealtime, and family devotional times. They need to take part in daily family worship beginning at a young age (Prov. 22:6). If children see us reading the Bible and praying often, they will learn to have their own time alone with God. Talking and praying together about decisions helps children apply Christian values to their own situations. For example, praying as a family about a car purchase teaches children to depend on God for guidance.

Paul's advice to Timothy applies well to parents: "Set an example for the believers in speech, in life, in love, in faith and in purity" (1 Tim. 4:12).

What daily situations in your life can serve as an opportunity to explain your faith to a child?

Non-Traditional Families

While the "traditional" family may be ideal, many people find themselves living in other family configurations.

Single Parents

Some parents find themselves alone, raising children without the aid of a spouse. Because it is hardly possible to be both mother and father, single parents have a much greater need for support from outside the home.

While the Bible doesn't specifically mention single parenting, it does give instructions about widows and orphans. A single parent is like a widow in that he or she has no partner to encourage and help with the many responsibilities of raising children. Children in single-parent homes, though not lacking both parents, miss the benefit of having both a mother and father.

Christians are continually asked to look after widows and orphans (Isa. 1:16–17; James 1:27). We're also told to carry each other's burdens (Gal. 6:2). Surely, that means that we should assist single parents when needed. That might include providing baby-sitting, home or car repairs, or financial assistance. Just listening to the mom of a teenager can be a big help.

Singles

Many people in our society are single, some never married, others divorced, and some widowed. While God created marriage for our benefit, the Bible also makes it clear that a single lifestyle is an acceptable—even desirable—option for some people (see 1 Cor. 7:1–17). Jesus, after all, was a single adult!

Single adults and those without children can play a significant role in the family life of others by offering assistance to single parents or serving as role models or mentors for young adults. The Apostle Paul was like an adopted father to Timothy. Paul's love and encouragement were no doubt instrumental in Timothy's becoming a pastor. It is not necessary to have children in order to be a godly influence on younger people.

List some ways you might help a single parent or young person that you know.

Protecting the Family

Families face many pressures today. Traditions that were once held dear are now challenged on every side. Families must be intentional about creating and protecting healthy homes. Several areas call for special attention.

The Priority of Marriage

After our relationship to God, marriage is the most important relationship that we have. It must come before parental responsibilities, household chores, and jobs. A couple needs time each day to be alone, discuss the events of the day, and express affection. Planning a regular "date" is important for married couples, whether it's going out for dinner or just taking a walk.

Proper Scheduling

Some common practices in our society can be destructive to family. One of them is busyness. Raising children involves juggling many activities, especially when young people begin to cultivate their own interests. Sports, television, friends, or computer time can crowd out family time. Parents must help children limit outside activities in order to allow adequate time for chores, homework, and especially family activities.

When family members are continually too busy to share a meal together, they are really allowing other things to usurp the place of family time. Busyness may appear to be normal, but it greatly hinders building family relationships.

Guarding Against Outside Influences

The values of our world can creep seductively into the home through television, the Internet, movies, music, and friends. Parents need to constantly monitor the family's input through these channels and be prepared to discuss the unhealthy concepts that will inevitably surface. Some television programs, CDs, unsupervised Internet time, or other forms of media may need to be eliminated entirely.

What video, movie, or television show has your family watched recently? What were the underlying values that it portrayed?

Controlling Spending

Materialism is a prominent influence in our society. The Bible teaches us to seek God's kingdom above all else (Matt. 6:33) and to trust God to supply our all needs (Phil. 4:19). By contrast, our culture places great emphasis on wealth and self-sufficiency.

Be wary of the materialism trap. Acquiring more things requires more money and usually more time away from home to earn it. It may be better to invest time in nurturing our children than in working to provide them with more things—especially things they don't need. A good alternative to spending money is to find a community service project that the family can do together. That will build your family through shared experience and model God's love for others.

What are some ministry projects you and your family might work together on?

Reflecting Christ

God created us to reflect His image in our relationships. The lasting loyalty of husband and wife mirrors God's faithfulness to us. As we submit to each other in love, we demonstrate Christ's love for the Church. A Christian home is built on love, respect, and care for one another. Children learn to model these qualities from parents who make their faith part of daily life. To protect the family unit, we must prioritize our time well and reject distracting influences. The home becomes the model of compassion in the body of Christ, the Church.

To Learn More

Alone with God: Biblical Inspiration for the Unmarried by Michael Warden

Dare to Discipline by James Dobson

Fighting For Your Marriage, by Howard Markman, Scott Stanley, and Susan L. Blumberg

The Five Love Languages of Children by Gary Chapman and Ross Campbell

Married Lovers Married Friends by Steve and Annie Chapman

Making Love Last Forever by Gary Smalley

Passion and Purity by Elisabeth Elliot

The Strong-Willed Child by James Dobson

All additional books and resources are available from Wesleyan Publishing House at www.wesleyan.org/wph or by calling 800.4.WESLEY (800.493.7539).

Personal Spiritual Journal

DATE _____

_____

_____

_____

_____

_____

_____

_____

_____

_____

_____

_____

_____

_____

My Prayer Today—

_____

_____

_____

_____

CHAPTER 6

Beside Still Waters

Key Passages of the Bible

> *The Lord is my shepherd, I shall not be in want.*
> —Psalm 23:1

> *As the Father has loved me, so have I loved you. Remain*
> *in my love."*
> —John 15:9

 **Bible Basics**

Psalm 23:1–6

Stanza One
¹The LORD is my shepherd, I shall not be in want.
²ᵃHe makes me lie down in green pastures,
²ᵇhe leads me beside quiet waters,
³ᵃhe restores my soul.
³ᵇHe guides me in paths of righteousness
³ᶜfor his name's sake.
⁴ᵃ,ᵇEven though I walk through the valley of the shadow of death
⁴ᶜI will fear no evil.

Centering line
⁴ᵈfor you are with me,
⁴ᵉyour rod and your staff,
⁴ᶠthey comfort me.

Stanza two

5aYou prepare a table before me

5bin the presence of my enemies.

5cYou anoint my head with oil;

5dmy cup overflows.

6aSurely goodness and love will follow me

6ball the days of my life,

6cand I will dwell in the house of the LORD

6dforever.

 ## Connecting God's Word to Life

Who is the person with whom this poem begins and ends? What assurances does this give the author (David), and what confidence does this person give you today?

Great Passages from the Bible

As disciples of Jesus Christ, we want to reflect His character in all that we are, do, and say. Reading and studying God's Word, our guide for life and faith, is the first step in doing that. The next step is to apply what we've learned to our daily lives. The two passages of Scripture in this chapter offer foundational insights about our relationship with God, His love for us, and the role we have in God's kingdom. Let's look at a couple of the great passages from the Bible, Psalm 23 and John 13–17.

Psalm 23 has been around for three thousand years now. These words have been a source of strength and calm assurance for the people of God—both Jewish and Christian—in times of crisis.

David, the author, uses images from his youth as a shepherd to portray God's constant care. He remembered that aspect of God's nature when he faced the giant, Goliath, when King Saul tried to kill him, when he fell victim to his lust for Bathsheba, when his own son, Absalom, staged a coup against him, and when he lay dying while two of his sons struggled over the soon-to-be vacant throne.

Name a situation in which you have known fear or disappointment.

Isaiah, Micah, and Ezekiel, among other prophets in the Old Testament have also recalled this image of God as a shepherd. In fact, Jacob expressed that idea to his son Joseph a thousand years before David's time. Jacob said: "God has been my shepherd all my life to this day" (Gen. 48:15).

Jesus picked up that same image in one of His parables (Luke 15:3–7) and in a sermon (John 10:1–18), declaring that He (Jesus) is the Good Shepherd. Even the final book of the Bible says that the Lamb, Jesus, will lead us like a shepherd to living waters (Rev. 7:17). So from Genesis to Revelation, God's relationship to His people is compared to that of a shepherd tending his flock.

In fact, the image of shepherd was frequently applied to leaders in the ancient world. If they were godly leaders, they were seen as reminders of God's care, protection, and wisdom.

The life of Jesus is the prime example of how a person's relationship with God brings the benefit of care and protection. The kind of trust in God that this psalm talks about characterized Jesus' life.

Can you think of times in Jesus' earthly life when even He might have relied on the assurance offered by the Twenty-third Psalm?

We Have a Relationship with God

In this psalm, God is referred to as the LORD. The word *LORD* is a translation of Hebrew word represented by the letters YHWH. This name for God first appears in Genesis 2, although a different, more general name for God is used in Genesis 1. Notice the ways these two chapters complement one another.

Genesis 1	Genesis 2
Creation of the World	Creation of the Garden
Creation of the Human Race	Creation of Adam
Creation of Animals	Adam Names Each Animal
No Responsibility Given	Adam Must Choose to Obey

God not only made the universe, including human beings, but also chose to enter into a relationship with Adam and Eve. Whenever the name YHWH is used in Genesis, there is the expectation that God will have a covenant relationship with people. So when David says, "The LORD [YHWH] is my Shepherd," he shows that he has a covenant relationship with God. It is in that relationship that David finds peace, restoration, guidance, courage, confidence, and hope.

Do you have a relationship with God? If so, what does that provide in your life?

David's Phrase	Your Paraphrase
Green Pastures	
Quiet Waters	
Paths of Righteousness	
Valley of the Shadow of Death	
Table in the Presence of Enemies	
My Cup Overflows	
Dwell in the House of the Lord	

Also, notice that David begins the Psalm writing about God in the third person, but in the centering line of the poem, he shifts to the second person—"you." It is as if he is not just affirming that there is a LORD, but he is talking directly with Him.

Knowing God personally should lead to conversation with Him. For example, reciting a creed, singing a hymn, or even reading this psalm can lead to personal intimacy with the Lord. That provides an opportunity for a "You and I" conversation. You can talk to God in a personal way, just as you do with other people!

Our Relationship Brings Confidence

Psalm 23 contains three statements of affirmation that begin with "I shall" or "I will." First, "I shall not be in want." God promises to meet our needs—for rest in green pastures, to drink from still waters, for restoration of our inner being, and for guidance in doing the right thing.

Second, David says, "I will not fear evil." Even when death or enemies threaten loved ones or us, the Lord is there to comfort and nourish us.

Finally, David says, "I will dwell in the house of the LORD forever." God will be with us always. Our covenant relationship with Him is forever. He is not fickle.

Describe a time when you needed to make one of these affirmations of certainty.

The words of the Twenty-third Psalm are powerful. On some occasions, people who were comatose have responded when pastors or family members whispered these words in their ears. Soldiers in battle have recited this psalm. Prisoners being led to execution are reminded of its words. Even when the crisis is not acute, David's words give perspective and assurance for everyday living. God inspired them, and now He inspires us through them.

Memorizing this psalm is a great idea. Put these words in your heart, and call on them whenever you need them.

 ## Bible Basics

Selections from John 13–17
John 13:34–35

> "A new command I give you: Love one another. As I have loved you, so you must love one another. By this all men will know that you are my disciples, if you love one another."

John 14:15–16a

"If you love me, you will obey what I command. And I will ask the Father, and he will give you another Counselor to be with you forever—the Spirit of truth."

John 14:23

"If anyone loves me, he will obey my teaching. My Father will love him, and we will come to him and make our home with him."

John 15:9

"As the Father has loved me, so have I loved you. Remain in my love."

John 16:27

"The Father himself loves you because you have loved me and have believed that I came from God."

John 17:25–26

"Righteous Father . . . I have made you known to them and will continue to make you known in order that the love you have for me may be in them and that I myself may be in them."

Connecting God's Word to Life

Based on these verses, list several words that characterize the relationship between the persons of the Trinity—Father, Son, and Holy Spirit.

Love and Obedience

Have you ever noticed that a loving person is able to make each person they know feel that he or she is a special object of affection? Jesus seemed to do that with His disciples. On the last night of His earthly life, Jesus spoke about love constantly. The early part of the Gospel of John, chapters 1–12, mentions love six times. But later, in John 13–17, love is mentioned 31 times. John speaks of himself as the "disciple whom Jesus loved." Jesus wants each of us to experience this sense of intimacy with Him.

He also wants us to share that sense of special connection with His other followers. In fact, Jesus went so far as to say that love is the distinctive mark of a disciple: "All men will know that you are my disciples, if you love one another" (John 13:35). What a great strategy for sharing God's love with others!

Notice that this is a command, not just a suggestion. Can love be commanded? Jesus thought so! Of course, He considered His disciples—including you and me— to be an extension of Himself. He is the vine; we are the branches.

Jesus promised that the Father would send another Counselor to be with the disciples forever—the Spirit of truth. In John 14:6, Jesus identifies Himself as the "truth." The Spirit will live on in us as we obey God. As John Calvin wrote and John Wesley lived, "All right knowledge of God is born of obedience."[1] This Spirit of truth is like breath that keeps us alive and like wind at our back, helping us to move forward new directions. Since Jesus and His words are the truth, the Spirit of Jesus lives in us as we obey His commands.

Name one thing you can do obey Jesus' command to love others.

Jesus Answers Questions

When traveling, many children and even adults frequently ask, "Are we there yet? How much further?" We followers of Christ sometimes ask those same questions on our journey of faith. The disciples wondered those very things in John 13, 14, and 16. Jesus used their questions to build their faith.

In the early part of chapter 13, John reveals that Jesus knew that the time had come for Him to leave this world and go to the Father. Jesus understood that the Father had placed all things under Jesus' power, and He wanted to show the disciples how much He loved them, so He began to wash the disciples' feet. Then, He patiently answered a series of questions, much like a father or mother would answer the child's question, "Are we there yet?"

Consider yourself as the one asking questions of Jesus in John 13. What do you learn from His replies?

Ref.	Question	Lesson
13:6	Lord, are you going to wash my feet?	
13:24	Ask him which one he means. . . . Lord who is it?	
13:36	Lord, where are you going?	
13:37	Lord, why can't I follow you now?	
14:5	Lord, we don't know where you are going, so how can we know the way?	
14:8	Lord, show us the Father and that will be enough for us.	
14:22	But, Lord, why do you intend to show yourself to us and not to the world?	
16:19	What does he mean by saying, "In a little while you will see me no more, and then after a little while you will see me," and "because I am going to the Father?" What does he mean by "a little while?"	

It was a sign of Jesus' love for His disciples that He took their questions seriously. The questions provided opportunity for their learning in a way that a sermon would not have. Peter learned that to follow Jesus meant to allow himself to be served by Jesus. He learned as well that the reason he could not go with Jesus yet was that his self-assurance had blinded him to his own capacity to deny Jesus. Thomas learned that Jesus was not so much about drawing a map to our destination as He himself is the destination, and our companion for the trip. Philip learned that to see Jesus is to see God the Father and that he can trust Jesus as the only way to God. Judas (not Iscariot) learned that God is best known by those who love Jesus enough to obey His teaching. In chapter 16, the disciples learned that following Jesus will lead to times of tears and grief, but on the other side of that sadness is joy.

Why did John include this question-and-answer period in his writing? Was he simply reporting the facts, or did he believe that future believers would need to know that asking questions is OK for a Christian? Also, did John perhaps think that both the questioner and those who listened might benefit form seeing that Jesus is with us during our times of doubt?

What would you like to ask Jesus?

Father, Son, and Holy Spirit

More than any other book in the Bible, the Gospel of John provides a foundation for the Christian belief that God is Triune—three in one. Although the term *Trinity* does not appear in the Scripture, the fact that God is Father, Son, and Holy Spirit is seen clearly in John 13–17. Understanding all aspects of this doctrine is not a requirement for being a Christian. You might not understand how a brown cow can eat green grass and give white milk that makes yellow butter, but it still tastes good! In the same way, believers benefit from the Trinity even if they can't explain it. We know that God is Father because we have met His Son, and it was the Son who told us of the Holy Spirit.

We believe that God the Father cannot be understood apart from the Son and the Holy Spirit, the Son cannot be understood apart from the Father and the Holy Spirit, and the Holy Spirit cannot be understood apart from the Father and the Son. We pray to the

Father in the name of the Son and are aided by the Holy Spirit as we pray. As an analogy, radio transmissions are all around us in the air. They come from a source (the Father) with an embedded message (the Son), and the message can be heard by means of a receiver (the Spirit). All three are essential for communicating with the one reality (God).

What messages from God are heard in John 13–17? Look at the beginning of John's gospel (1:1–18) and then return to John 13:1–4; 14:6–11, 15–17; 15:26–27; 16:7, 15; and 17:1–5, 24. In the entire Old Testament there are fewer than ten references to God as Father, but there are more than fifteen such references in the three chapters of Jesus' Sermon on the Mount (Matt. 5–7). In John 15–17, there are also many references to God as Father, as well as Son and Holy Spirit.

What do you learn about God from the scriptures noted above?

Love, Questions, and God as Trinity

Jesus communicates a number of things in John 13–17. We've looked primarily at three of them: His message of love, His patient willingness to answer questions, and His understanding of the relationship between His Father, the Holy Spirit, and Himself. What do we learn from these important messages?

First, we learn that Jesus loves His disciples. This love is not just a command of Jesus; we see it in His words and actions. He washed the disciples' feet, prepared them for His departure, and went not only the second mile for them but also the last mile. He wanted them to know that the sacrifice He would make was caused not by His spiteful enemies or the Devil but from the love of the Father. This is a rigorous love that appears to be a "frowning providence" but which actually hides a "smiling face." Tough times do not mean that God has deserted us. They can be a pathway to a glorious purpose and bring the glorious presence of God. Jesus gave His disciples the promise that the Spirit would come if He returned to the Father.

Second, we learn that Jesus loves His disciples enough to answer to their questions. The relationship of a believer to the Lord is a real one. Perhaps the first disciples should already have understood the things they asked about. Perhaps the stress of their impending separation from their teacher caused them to forget some things. Whatever the case, Jesus answered their queries as they arose. For present-day believers, many questions are already answered in the Bible—both in the Old and New Testaments. Jesus, the Word behind those words, answers many questions through the written record. And He has also asked the Father to send the Holy Spirit to guide us, not only as individuals but also as the body of Christ, the Church.

One example of this loving instruction is found in John 19:25–27, where Jesus entrusts Mary, His own grieving mother, and John, one of the grieving disciples, into one another's care. "From that very hour" John took Mary into his household. Much of the New Testament emphasizes this "one another" relationship. The fellowship of the Church is one way God answers our questions when we wonder, "Where does life go from here?"

A third lesson is that before there was a created world, there was love. Love is not just a command or a concept; it is grounded in the eternal relationship of the Trinity. Later on, in his first letter, John writes, "God is love" (1 John 4:8b). Love is the very essence of who God is.

In his Gospel, John repeatedly describes himself as "the disciple whom Jesus loved." What a great self-concept! That intimacy results from an intentional relationship. When we choose to obey the commands of Jesus, we are caught up into the fellowship of the Trinity—Christ in us, we in Him.

As a believer, you have a personal relationship with the Living God. In what ways does that relationship affect the way you live every day?

To Learn More

The Gospel of John (The Daily Study Bible Series) by William Barclay

John: a Bible Commentary in the Wesleyan Tradition by Joseph Dongell

Psalms: a Bible Commentary in the Wesleyan Tradition by Steven Lennox

A Shepherd Looks at the Twenty-third Psalm by Philip Keller

All additional books and resources are available from Wesleyan Publishing House at www.wesleyan.org/wph or by calling 800.4.WESLEY (800.493.7539).

Personal Spiritual Journal

DATE _____

_____

_____

_____

_____

_____

_____

_____

_____

_____

_____

_____

_____

My Prayer Today—

_____

_____

_____

_____

CHAPTER 7

The Hardest Lesson

Suffering

*But those who suffer he delivers in their suffering; he
speaks to them in their affliction.*

—Job 36:15

 **Bible Basics**

2 Corinthians 1:3–7

> [3]Praise be to the God and Father of our Lord Jesus Christ, the Father of
> compassion and the God of all comfort, [4]who comforts us in all our troubles,
> so that we can comfort those in any trouble with the comfort we ourselves
> have received from God. [5]For just as the sufferings of Christ flow over into our
> lives, so also through Christ our comfort overflows. [6]If we are distressed, it is
> for your comfort and salvation; if we are comforted, it is for your comfort,
> which produces in you patient endurance of the same sufferings we suffer.
> [7]And our hope for you is firm, because we know that just as you share in our
> sufferings, so also you share in our comfort.

1 Peter 4:12–16

> [12]Dear friends, do not be surprised at the painful trial you are suffering, as
> though something strange were happening to you. [13]But rejoice that you

participate in the sufferings of Christ, so that you may be overjoyed when his glory is revealed. [14]If you are insulted because of the name of Christ, you are blessed, for the Spirit of glory and of God rests on you. [15]If you suffer, it should not be as a murderer or thief or any other kind of criminal, or even as a meddler. [16]However, if you suffer as a Christian, do not be ashamed, but praise God that you bear that name.

 Connecting God's Word to Life

Based on these scriptures, would you say that suffering is a good thing or a bad thing? Why?

The Reality of Suffering

Several years ago, Dr. Paul Brand, a longtime medical missionary to India and pioneer in the treatment of leprosy, published a book entitled *Pain, the Gift Nobody Wants*. Dr. Brand's interesting view of pain resulted from his research into leprosy, a disease that often results in the absence of feeling in various parts of the patient's body. This absence of feeling, or anesthesia, frequently resulted in complications that were difficult to treat. Ordinarily, we think of freedom from pain as a blessing, and we search for ways to alleviate the discomfort of suffering. In fact, pain can be valuable since it indicates the presence of a disease or injury. God allows our suffering, even though we would rather He didn't!

Suffering in any form attracts our attention quickly and causes us to seek relief. Generally, it indicates a problem in one of three areas: body, spirit, or mind.

Physical	Spiritual	Emotional
Illness	Sin	Abuse
Injury	Guilt	Rejection
Hunger	Unforgiveness	Depression
Persecution	Separation from God	Regret

Causes of Suffering

Physical suffering may result from illness, injury, or hunger. Or it may result from factors outside the self, such as neglect, abuse, or persecution. When we identify a physical source for suffering, we seek medical treatment. Too often, there is no easy solution to a physical problem and the sufferer must endure pain.

Spiritual suffering results from sin and the guilt that it produces. This may be a more frequent cause of discomfort—even physical discomfort—than we choose to admit. We read in 1 Cor. 6:19–20: "Do you not know that your body is the temple of the Holy Spirit whom you have received from God? You are not your own; you are bought at a price. Therefore, honor God with your body." Pain produced by spiritual trauma has no medical cure. It needs a spiritual solution.

Some suffering has an emotional cause. The trauma experienced, for example, by an abused child is impossible to measure. Physical or relational distress can produce emotional suffering that continues even after the source of pain is removed. Those who have experienced this type of suffering have found that the promises of God's Word can provide healing.

> Pain produced by spiritual trauma has no medical cure. It needs a spiritual solution.

In each of these cases, a ready cure for suffering may be available. Medical treatment may alleviate physical suffering. Confession, repentance, and forgiveness are the cure for spiritual suffering. Medical and psychological treatments can often relieve emotional distress.

But there are times when suffering cannot be relieved; it must be endured. What then?

Which cause of suffering—physical, spiritual, or emotional— is the most difficult for you to deal with? Why?

Biblical Examples of Suffering

When we think of suffering, the biblical character Job immediately comes to mind. It would be hard to name anyone, except Christ Himself, who suffered more than Job. Yet when even his own wife advised him to curse God and die, Job replied, "You are talking like a foolish woman. Shall we accept good from God and not trouble?" Job's reply shows that it's possible to endure suffering, with God's help.

David recognized that "the LORD is a refuge for the oppressed, a stronghold in time of trouble" (Ps. 9:9) and that "in the day of trouble, He will keep me safe in His dwelling. He will hide me in the shelter of His tabernacle and set me high upon a rock" (Ps. 27:5).

Jesus Himself is our ultimate example of suffering. It's difficult to imagine the terrible physical, mental, and spiritual anguish He endured on the Cross. Yet He endured that pain for our salvation. He was able to face the gravest moment of suffering, death, in triumph.

Scripture shows us that suffering is a reality and that we can endure it through faith in God.

Purpose of Suffering

What purpose is there in this pain? Why do we suffer? Conventional wisdom proposes that good things happen to good people while the bad things are reserved for bad people. As you survey your list of family members, friends, and acquaintances, you quickly discover that conventional wisdom in this instance is not entirely right. The Apostle Peter wrote, "Dear friends, do not be surprised at the painful trial you are suffering, as though something strange were happening to you. But rejoice that you participate in the sufferings of Christ, so that you may be overjoyed when his glory is revealed" (1 Pet. 4:12–13).

To the Christian, the experience of suffering is meaningful. In fact, suffering was the instrument that God chose for our redemption. Consider Paul's writing to the Colossians about the Christ and His work:

> [19]For God was pleased to have all his fullness dwell in him, [20]and through him to reconcile to himself all things, whether things on earth or things in heaven, by making peace through his blood, shed on the cross. [21]Once you were alienated from God and were enemies in your minds because of your evil behavior. [22]But now he has reconciled you by Christ's physical body through death to present you holy in his sight, without blemish and free from accusation (Col. 1:19–22).

Jesus came so that He could suffer and so that you and I could be reconciled. In fact, that is the only way that you and I could be saved!

The Apostle Peter goes a step further, saying that our own suffering plays a role in our Christian development. "Therefore, since Christ suffered in his body, arm yourselves also with the same attitude, because he who has suffered in his body is done with sin" (1 Pet. 4:1). Suffering, then, is not entirely bad but can be a good thing because it helps to improve our faith. Listen to the Apostle James:

> Suffering is not entirely bad. It can be a good thing because it helps to improve our faith.

> [2]Consider it pure joy, my brothers, whenever you face trials of many kinds, [3]because you know that the testing of your faith develops perseverance. [4]Perseverance must finish its work so that you may be mature and complete, not lacking anything (James 1:2–4).

The writer of Hebrews adds, "Endure hardship as discipline; God is treating you as sons. For what son is not disciplined by his father?" (Heb. 12:7).

God allows us to suffer because suffering forces us to realize our helplessness and depend upon God. The great Christian writer C. S. Lewis referred to pain as the megaphone of God. God shouts to us in our pain, cutting through our conceit and self-centeredness. As we experience suffering, our faith is increased as we learn to depend upon Him.

At times, the link between our suffering and our faith may be obvious. Financial loss, for example, may very quickly cause us to depend upon God and discover that He is faithful to provide. At other times, it may be difficult to see a direct benefit or "happy ending" to every painful situation. As we trust God, however, and grow more mature, we may look back and see that God has been working for our good at all times—even when life seemed to be at its worst. As the Apostle Paul promised, "Being confident of this, that he who began a good work in you will carry it on to completion until the day of Christ Jesus" (Phil. 1:6).

What has caused pain in your life recently? Can you see that God is at work in your suffering? How so?

Coping with Suffering

We cannot control what happens to us. But every one of us can control his or her response. Your attitude will largely determine how you cope with suffering. As it is in most areas of life, when you suffer, attitude is everything.

So how do we face suffering? Here are five steps for dealing with suffering. For those who suffer, they are steppingstones to spiritual growth.

Avoid It

Two small brothers were playing in the yard when they accidentally stirred up a nest of yellow jackets. The older brother went screaming to his mother in pain! After care and comfort were administered to him, the younger brother, having stood silently by while his brother was treated, quietly said to his mother, "I got stung too!"

Sometimes we suffer because we needlessly endure pain or inflict it upon ourselves. It is obvious advice but still good: Avoid suffering if you can.

God has created us wonderfully. Our bodies are a gift from Him and in fact are

His temple (1 Cor. 6:19). We can avoid needless pain by honoring God with our lives. He's given us plenty of guidance on doing that. By eating well, resting as God commands us to, avoiding sexual immorality and harmful substances such as alcoholic beverages, tobacco, and illicit drugs, we greatly improve our enjoyment of life.

Relating to God and others honestly and lovingly will help to avoid spiritual and emotional suffering as well. When we confess sin, we're freed from guilt. When we follow Jesus' "Golden Rule" and treat others as we'd like to be treated (Luke 6:31), we have healthier relationships. The advice is simple but true: Life goes better when lived God's way.

Can you think of an instance when you brought pain upon yourself? What did you learn from the experience?

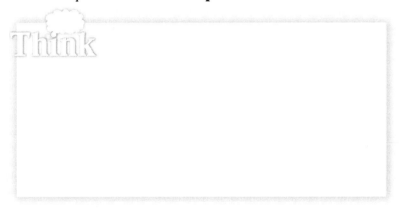

Be Honest

Next, be honest about your suffering. That involves first defining what suffering is and making a distinction between genuine suffering and a simple interruption in an otherwise comfortable life.

Some of us seem to thrive on crisis. It is as if life revolves around a series of painful events that we must patiently endure. Often, these "traumatic" events are just the routines of daily life—a missed stoplight or a spoiled dinner. That's not suffering.

Real suffering does exist, however, even in the relative comfort of North American society. For some it is a chronic illness. For others it may be pain inflicted by abuse or neglect. For others it may be hurt brought on by their own doing, such as poor financial planning, failed relationships, or destructive habits resulting in failed health. Even self-inflicted suffering is real and painful. And it is important to Christ. So the next step in being honest about suffering is to be honest before God about your pain.

David's cry in Psalm 22 is a powerful example of the fact that we are free to bring our pain before God in honest lamentation. It begins with the very words that Christ later spoke on the cross, "My God, my God, why have you forsaken me?" The psalmist goes on to paint a graphic picture of suffering and pain at the hands of the ungodly. Both David and Christ used these words to pour out their pain before the Father. You can do the same.

What is the difference between suffering and inconvenience?

Trust God

Too often, we blame God for our pain rather than looking to Him for help and comfort. While God allows suffering, He is still good. It was human sin that initiated suffering. God remains willing to redeem us, even using suffering in the process.

When we suffer, our thoughts quickly center on ourselves and often take an accusatory tone toward God.

- Why is this happening to me?
- Is this what I get for trying to be good?
- If God cared about me, He'd never let this happen.

Rather than accuse God, simply admit your sorrow to Him and seek His comfort, guidance, and relief. Christ's purpose in suffering was to redeem us. Our purpose is to be fully reconciled to Him. Therefore the best result of suffering is that we would simply focus more of our attention on Christ.

Because we live in an instant age, we tend to believe that we should have instant understanding of all that is happening to us. When we don't see immediate solutions, we become angry. But there are some things we simply will not understand until we get to heaven. In the meantime, we trust God—even when we suffer. At the height of one of his own personal tests, the great missionary Hudson Taylor wrote: "It doesn't matter how great the pressure is. What really matters is where the pressure lies, whether it comes between me and God or whether it presses me nearer His heart."

When we are pressed near the heart of God, He is faithful and He will hold us. Jesus said, "Therefore I tell you, do not worry about your life, what you will eat or drink; or about your body, what you will wear" (Matt. 6:25). We can entrust our souls to a faithful Creator. Few feelings compare with the joy of watching God step in and solve a problem that seems impossible. When you suffer, ask for God's help, then wait for Him to provide what He thinks best—whether it's relief from suffering, an important lesson of faith, or simply the ability to endure.

During the short term, God is faithful and we can depend upon Him. When you are tempted to lose hope, remember that God has not abandoned you.

What would you say to a friend whose suffering has caused him or her to lose faith in God?

Focus on the Eternal

Because God is faithful does not necessarily mean that our suffering will quickly disappear. Our Lord's agenda for us is full of surprises and unexpected twists.

When we suffer, we may resist God's attempts to redirect our lives and look for ways to cope on our own. When trials linger and you begin to wear down, Satan will make all kinds of suggestions. He will even give you evidence that other people were able to run away from what you have to endure. He will call you to question God's integrity. He'll point to many ways that you can avoid suffering by breaking faith with God.

When that happens, take the long view. Focus on the eternal glory that God has in store for us. Warren Wiersbe describes this long view of suffering:

Suffering and *glory* are twin truths that are woven into the fabric of Peter's letter. The world believes that the absence of suffering means glory, but a Christian's outlook is different. The trial of our faith today is the assurance of glory when Jesus returns . . . This was the experience of our Lord . . . and it shall be our experience. But it is necessary to understand that God is not going to replace suffering with glory; rather He will transform suffering into glory."

God is busy with us, shaping us and using suffering as an instrument. The final goal for all of us is that we can be made into the image of our Lord Jesus Christ. The Apostle Paul gave us this wonderful promise: "And we know that in all things God works for the good of those who love him, who have been called according to his purpose" (Rom. 8:28). Yet we need to hear the following verse as well: "For those God foreknew he also predestined to be conformed to the likeness of his Son" (Rom. 8:29). The ultimate goal for every Christian is to become like Christ. Though there surely will be some progress toward that goal in this life, the final realization will occur in the endless ages that we will spend with Him.

From time to time, all of us need to face the marvelous truth that we are just "pilgrims in a weary land," and that "this world is not my home." God is preparing us to live with the King of Kings and Lord of Lords. In a very real sense, living here is a preparation for eternal life. How nearsighted we can be!

List some good things that may result from your suffering.

Reach Out

One way that we can learn and thrive even in the midst of suffering is to elevate our vision beyond ourselves and our pain to minister to others. It was Paul who suggested that because of his chains, many were turned to Christ. Can our "chains" have that same effect? Certainly not as long as our focus is on the chains themselves. The more we focus on self, the more saturated our minds become with our own hurts and the less we are able to think of anything but our own plight.

If, however, our focus is on the higher purpose to which we have been called in Christ, we can accomplish good things, even in our suffering! Robert C. Bradford relates a story that happened to his family following World War II. They were living in southern California where Japanese-Americans at that time were experiencing great suffering because of feelings the war had left behind. The Bradford's neighbors were a Christian, Japanese-American family. The mother of this family was shy, modest, and compassionate. She knew that Robert's wife was ill but felt she could not come to their home to share her concern.

> To thrive in the midst of suffering, elevate your vision beyond self and pain to minister to others.

She did, however, always manage to meet Robert when he took out the trash. She would inquire about his wife's health and tell him that she was praying for her each day. Often she would present some food she had prepared for the couple. After several of these encounters, Mr. Bradford asked how she always managed to be on hand to offer her concern. She blushed and said, "I listen for the rattle of your garbage can."

As a new Christian, Bradford was inspired by the way she reached out even in the midst of her own suffering. She did not allow prejudice, modesty, or inconvenience to hold her back from reaching out in some small way to someone else with a need. She could have looked at that need and rationalized that her own suffering was far greater and that she needed to mind her own business and take care of herself. She didn't measure the suffering of others against her own suffering. She just saw a need and met it.

Recall David's lamentation in Psalm 22. In verse 22, the poem takes a dramatic turn away from David's inner pain to express a sense of purpose and direction. As David looks at the wonders of God, he is thankful. Finally, he says, "For he has not despised or disdained the suffering of the afflicted one; he has not hidden his face from him but has listened to his cry for help. From you comes my praise in the great assembly; before those who fear you will I fulfill my vows" (Ps. 22:24–25).

Is it possible that David discovered a purpose in suffering? Can you? When we concentrate on God and others instead of ourselves, we can find meaning in spite of our suffering.

Although we may not be able to change our circumstance, we can control our attitude toward them. As we cultivate a servant's attitude, we discover that suffering does not have the last word!

Name a way in which you might help another person in spite of what you have suffered—or because of it.

To Learn More

God's Healing for Your Trauma by Jerry Brecheisen

Holiness for Hurting People by David L. Thompson with Gina Thompson Eickhoff

Hope for the Troubled Heart by Billy Graham

The Problem of Pain by C. S. Lewis

Voice of the Martyrs website www.persecution.com

All additional books and resources are available from Wesleyan Publishing House at www.wesleyan.org/wph or by calling 800.4.WESLEY (800.493.7539).

Personal Spiritual Journal

DATE _____

_____

_____

_____

_____

_____

_____

_____

_____

_____

_____

_____

_____

_____

_____

My Prayer Today—

_____

_____

_____

_____

CHAPTER 8

Battling the Devil

Spiritual Warfare

> *For our struggle is not against flesh and blood, but against
> the rulers, against the authorities, against the powers of this
> dark world and against the spiritual forces of evil in the
> heavenly realms.*
>
> —Ephesians 6:12

 **Bible Basics**

Ephesians 6:10–18

[10]Finally, be strong in the Lord and in his mighty power. [11]Put on the full armor
of God so that you can take your stand against the devil's schemes. [12]For our
struggle is not against flesh and blood, but against the rulers, against the
authorities, against the powers of this dark world and against the spiritual
forces of evil in the heavenly realms. [13]Therefore put on the full armor of God,
so that when the day of evil comes, you may be able to stand your ground,
and after you have done everything, to stand. [14]Stand firm then, with the belt
of truth buckled around your waist, with the breastplate of righteousness in
place, [15]and with your feet fitted with the readiness that comes from the gospel
of peace. [16]In addition to all this, take up the shield of faith, with which you
can extinguish all the flaming arrows of the evil one. [17]Take the helmet of
salvation and the sword of the Spirit, which is the word of God. [18]And pray
in the Spirit on all occasions with all kinds of prayers and requests. With this

in mind, be alert and always keep on praying for all the saints.

 ## Connecting God's Word to Life

Who are the rulers, authorities, and other powers in your life?
Where are your spiritual battles to be fought?

The Reality of Spiritual Warfare

Spiritual warfare is real. Spiritual battles are fought not only in heaven and hell but also in the hearts and minds of human beings. Spiritual contests take place wherever the souls of people are at stake.

There are perhaps two dangers in dealing with the subject of spiritual warfare. One is that the reality of evil might be minimized—that we might deny the existence of such things as witchcraft, demonic possession, or the occult. Such things are very real and must be taken seriously. The other danger, however, is that we might become overly concerned with those activities and ignore the very real spiritual battles that take place in our own minds and homes every day.

That is probably the greater danger. Since activities such as witchcraft or the occult are clearly evil, the simple way to deal with them is to avoid them. It's in other areas that Satan is likely to direct his forces. The Bible suggests that he is often indirect, subtle, and devious in his assaults and may even "masquerade as an angel of light" (2 Cor. 11:14). Consequently, spiritual battles will be fought in ourselves, in our homes, in our communities, in our churches—indeed, in any situation where good people are found.

Yes, we should be concerned about satanic cults, witchcraft, and the like. These typically become battlefields for people who have been led into them gradually, dabbling with such things as Ouija boards or astrology. Some Christians are enamored by the weird, the spectacular, or the occult, treating them as entertainment. As a result, they gradually come to accept things that are contrary to the faith. Believers in Christ should have nothing to do with overt evil. As the Bible says, "God is light; in him there is no darkness at all" (1 John 1:5).

Yet as the well-know southern philosopher *Pogo* has said, "We have met the enemy and he is us!" The primary spiritual battle that you face is the battle within you—the battle for the self.

Spiritual Self-defense

Since we are eternal creatures only in the spiritual sense, it is interesting that so many people pay little attention to anything but the temporary features of themselves—the body and the mind. It's easy to become so focused on mental, emotional, and physical life that that we give little or no attention to our spiritual selves. That leaves us ill prepared to cope with the inevitable battle for the spiritual self. Many of us don't even recognize that there is a war going on.

The renowned psychiatrist Sigmund Freud believed that the two most important issues in human behavior were the aggressive instinct and sex. Other psychologists believe that altruistic tendencies are most important in explaining our behavior. Still others see human beings as basically depraved; and yet others, including B. F. Skinner, have seen human beings as a blank slate on which experience will write.

All of those explanations of human nature overlook spirituality. As Christians, we know that we are primarily and eternally spiritual creatures. We are also complex physical, mental, and emotional beings, yet we are primarily spiritual. Therefore, our spiritual development and care are most important.

Of course it is imperative that we give attention to all of our needs. We must develop and care for our minds and our bodies. Careful preparation in spirit, mind, and body will arm us for the battles that have eternal consequences. We must pay attention to the mind-body-spirit interaction if we are to be triumphant in spiritual warfare.

> Careful preparation in spirit, mind, and body arms us for battles that have eternal consequences.

Spiritual Care

Conflict among the physical, emotional, intellectual, and spiritual selves is common. The apostle Paul referred to this inner warfare when he wrote:

> [21]So I find this law at work: When I want to do good, evil is right there with me. [22]For in my inner being I delight in God's law; [23]but I see another law at work in the members of my body, waging war against the law of my mind and making me a prisoner of the law of sin at work in my members" (Rom. 7:21–23).

In this passage, Paul talks about the continual battle within, which he cannot win in his own strength. He goes on to describe how victory may be won through the power of Christ living within. The resources for this inner spiritual conflict and for spiritual warfare in a hostile world are identical. These battles are won "'not by might nor by power, but by my Spirit,' says the LORD Almighty" (Zech. 4:6).

Paul described the "armor" for this spiritual battle in Ephesians, chapter 6. The combat boots are *readiness*. The shield is *faith*. The "helmet" is *salvation*. The body armor is *righteousness*. And the offensive weapon, the sword of the Spirit, is the Word of God.

Uses of Spiritual Armor				
	Self	**Home**	**Comunity**	**Church**
Belt of Truth	Personal Integrity	Valuing Others	Public Integrity	Intolerance of False Teaching
Breastplate of Righteousness	Good Intentions	Treating Everyone Fairly	Social Justice	Inclusiveness
Shoes of the Gospel of Peace	Composure	Willingness to Settle Disputes	Community Involvement	Compassion Ministry
Sheild of Faith	Consistent Belief	Family Worship	Faith-based Decision Making	Truth Valued over Personal Comfort
Helmet of Salvation	Assurance of Relationship with God	Witnessing to Children	Sharing the Faith with Others	Evangelistic Ministry
Sword of Truth (God's Word)	Knowledge	Teaching Children about the Faith	Biblically Authentic Lifestyle	Consistent Bible Teaching

Knowing that we face spiritual battles, we must arm ourselves by actively strengthening our spiritual selves and becoming well versed in the Scriptures. Daily equipping is essential. Reading God's Word, communing with Him in prayer and meditation, affiliating with others who are committed to the same way of being, these are essential to dealing with spiritual conflict.

What are you doing to arm yourself for spiritual battle?

Physical Care

This is not to say that Christians should focus on spiritual issues to the neglect the others. We must also deal with psychological and physical issues if we are to be at our best spiritually. Some people are defeated spiritually as a consequence of neglecting their physical and psychological well being. Perhaps you have heard of some folk who reject medical care in the name of spirituality. They believe that accepting medical intervention for physical problems amounts to a denial of faith. While we know that God does miraculously heal, we also believe that He intends for us to do what we can—including making use of medical science—to care for our own bodies.

Neglect of our physical needs is poor preparation for spiritual warfare. It's important to eat properly, rest, and preserve our physical health as best we can. Physical health is an advantage in spiritual combat.

Psychological Care

We must also attend to our psychological selves. The lines between physical and psychological issues are sometimes ill defined. For example, the need for regular, adequate, quality sleep is absolutely essential to good psychological function. Many experts believe that sleep deficiencies underlie an array of mental and physical problems that represent the major preventable health issues in our world today. It is interesting that so many people worry about poor sleep only when it interferes with other routines, as in the case of insomnia. The number one problem in this area is that people simply don't *regularly* allot themselves their needed quantity of sleep, thereby accumulating a sleep debt that can have devastating consequences physically, psychologically, and spiritually.

It is essential that we give proper care to all our needs if we are to be triumphant spiritually. Depressed Christians are always prime targets for the enemy of their spiritual selves, and we know that people are more likely to be depressed if they neglect their physical and psychological health.

What is the current state of your physical and emotional health? In what ways might that affect your spiritual well being?

Spiritual Battlegrounds

To be sure, not all spiritual battles are inner conflicts. There are outside forces that will attempt to destroy us. These need not be spectacular. The enemy of our eternal souls will use the most ordinary, mundane things to defeat us spiritually. People, places, and things may all be turned to the advantage of Satan. There is no such thing as being so spiritual as to escape the efforts of the dark forces of evil to overthrow us. Think about Job! This most righteous man of his time became the target of the Devil. His life became a battleground for a cosmic struggle between good and evil.

Jesus said that we are to be the salt in society. He pointed to the reality that the world is a hostile place and that we must penetrate it for good. When we do that, we engage in spiritual warfare, taking Christ's redeeming presence into all the places we go. By affirming Christian values, practicing a Christian lifestyle, and showing Christ's love to others in every place we inhabit, we engage the world for God—we do spiritual warfare!

Here are some of the places where you might find yourself engaged in spiritual battle.

The Home

The home may be battleground in spiritual warfare; and often, the battle there is lost. Even Christian homes sometimes fall prey to the forces of spiritual darkness. Adultery, the abuse or neglect of children, and divorce are realities even in the Christian community.

> A strong marriage is a good defense in the battle for the home.

One reason for the spiritual collapse of a home is the surrender of moral authority by the father. In too many cases, a father may be absent during the critical developmental years of children. In about two thirds of the cases brought to juvenile court, no father is present in the home. Men must be spiritual leaders for their children (Prov. 23:22–24).

Marriage is another point of spiritual conflict. Given the prevailing attitude toward marital fidelity in our culture, Christian spouses must spend extra effort building and preserving strong marriages. By undermining a marriage, Satan affects many people—the couple, their children, and extended family members. Building a strong marriage is a defense in the battle for the home.

Entertainment

Entertainment is another point of spiritual conflict. Television, movies, popular music, magazines, videos, video games, CDs, MP3 players, the Internet—the number of entertainment channels that are available to us is staggering. Unfortunately, Satan has turned many of these to his advantage, bombarding us and our children with ungodly messages and temptation.

No form of communication is evil in itself, yet Christians must be savvy in their use of the entertainment media. Here are some questions to consider when choosing entertainment:

- What is the underlying message? Does it reinforce my spiritual disciplines or undermine them?
- How much time will I spend doing this? Is that a wise use of my time?
- Are there alternatives that would better support my desire to keep a pure mind, heart, and body?
- What place does entertainment have in my life? Is that appropriate?

Peer pressure among children and teenagers is perhaps stronger today than ever. Parents are often afraid that they will be viewed negatively by their children for censoring entertainment. Yet isn't it reasonable to assume that our spiritual enemies will take advantage of this battlefield? It is better to risk the wrath of our children than to lose them. We must use entertainment wisely if we are to remain spiritually fit.

About how many hours a week do you spend using various entertainment media? Do you think your use of entertainment is balanced? If not, what change will you make?

Substance Abuse

Drugs—legal and illegal—are a part of everyday life in North America. Each of us probably knows someone whose life has been ruined by chemical abuse. For the most part, we are exposed to these temptations out in the community, not at church. Some Christians, however, seem to minimize the danger of substance abuse by modeling behaviors that set a poor example.

Nicotine addiction is now considered a psychiatric disorder, listed in the same sections of a diagnostic manual as marijuana and cocaine. Many people believe that beer is a relatively benign beverage, yet it is the drink of choice for most alcoholics. We are perhaps so concerned about dramatic new problems that we have overlooked some of the old ones—things that Satan still uses to ensnare people.

Avoidance of harmful substances continues to be the only sure way to have spiritual victory over them. Proponents of the lottery have been known to say, "You can't win if you don't play." When it comes to addictive substances, you can't lose if you don't use.

Do any of your lifestyle habits represent a danger to your spiritual life? If so, what will you do about them?

Wealth and Possessions

We live in a scientific age. Modern technology is developing so quickly that before we've mastered the use of one gadget, a better one comes along!

It's tempting to be caught up in the "must have" mentality of our world. That way of thinking is a trap that Satan uses to distract us from the things that really matter. Jesus once told of a wealthy man who became engrossed in the search to "have it all." As soon as he filled one barn with goods, he planned to tear it down and build a bigger one. Bigger, more, better, faster. His philosophy of life was similar to the consumer mind-set that tempts us. In the story, God confronted the man, saying, "You fool! This very night your life will be demanded from you. Then who will get what you have prepared for yourself?" (Luke 12:20).

Satan wants to keep our attention on ourselves. Tempting us with the desire for wealth and possessions is a great way to do that. Being spiritually fit means taking a God-view of things—seeing them as tools to accomplish a purpose, not trinkets that bring satisfaction.

Is your view of things in line with God's? These questions may help you decide.

- Do I spend more time with things or with people?
- Am I more concerned about my retirement account or my relationship with God?
- How often do I say, "I've *got* to have that!"?
- How many things do I have that I know I don't need?

The Occult

Rationalism is the dominant philosophy of this scientific age, and it often leaves no space for spiritual concerns. Is it any wonder that many people are so attracted to false religions? Rationalism doesn't meet their needs for real meaning in life.

Sidney Jourard, in his book *Healthy Personality*, says, "Man is incurably religious. What varies among men is what they are religious about." There are many people who claim to be rationalists, perhaps even naturalists, who are fascinated by stories of ghosts, demons, possession, devils, and witches. In the days when people accepted the spirit world without much question, we may

> Christians must be aware of the occult and be on guard against it.

have been better prepared to deal with such things. Now that we are accustomed to seeing a cause-and-effect explanation for everything in life, we may be more vulnerable to attacks from the dark world.

Christians must be aware of the occult and be on guard against it. We have no cause for alarm because Jesus Christ is Lord over all the world, including demonic forces. Yet dark forces do have power in the world and can ensnare the unwary. That's why believers in Christ avoid witchcraft in all of its forms (Gal. 5:20). Even things that seem harmless, such as Ouija boards, tarot cards, fantasy role-playing, and astrology can be dangerous in that they open the door to contact with the demonic world.

Worship

From time to time, people get caught up in all sorts of marginal activities in the name of worship. People have done the most bizarre things—including snake handling, drinking poison, and handling fire—believing that they were authentic expressions of Christian worship. Some believe that truly spiritual worship always involves some sort of highly charged emotional activity. Emotion, of course, is an element in most spiritual experiences. In those cases, however, emotion is the *effect* of spirituality, not the cause.

We're not likely to see snake handling in church these days, but emotional arousal is often used as a substitute for genuine worship. In that way, emotional experience becomes an end in itself. The danger in that is that people are much more vulnerable to the power of suggestion when they are emotionally aroused. The forces of evil can take advantage of those who are in a state of near emotional frenzy.

The Cult of Celebrity

Our culture loves celebrities. Interestingly, when people are well known, we become interested in their opinions about nearly everything. We want to know what breakfast cereal a star athlete eats, and we avidly listen to relationship advice given by movie stars. Celebrities influence everything from our clothing styles to our political opinions.

Yet celebrities are often nonbelievers and may hold un-Christian—even anti-Christian—views on matters of faith and family. Too often, celebrities model a lifestyle that glorifies self-adulation and self-indulgence.

To remain spiritually fit, we must choose Christian role models. Carefully evaluate the lifestyle and message of those whom you honor with your respect and attention.

Who are your role models? Why do you choose to model yourself after them?

Taking the Offensive

Our spiritual warfare is not to be defensive only. Remember the old sports adage, "The best defense is a good offense!" We put on the whole armor of God not to just protect ourselves, but to destroy evil as well. Christians are to be salt and light (see Matt. 5:13–16), penetrating the darkness in our communities and engaging evil where we find it.

Sometimes we're timid about doing that. One local ministerial association became publicly opposed the establishment of another liquor store in its community. At the meeting where they voiced their opposition, the man who proposed opening the store asked them, "Where have you guys been before now? I've been selling bootleg liquor in this community for years and I've never heard a complaint from any of you." Where had they been?

Yet many believers are active in penetrating the darkness around them. I know of a pastor who sought out and lovingly cared for a human derelict in his community who was dying of AIDS at a time when few people would go near sufferers of that condition. He touched, fed, clothed, and transported the man until his death. That pastor claimed a spiritual victory by showing compassion on the man and leading him to the Lord.

Compassion is our motivation for offensive spiritual warfare. Having been freed from the power of darkness, we want to free others as well. Evangelism, social activism, and even political lobbying are ways that we can change our communities for the better. In the matter of spiritual warfare, there can be no pacifists. Doing nothing for God in the world amounts to a victory for the enemy. As believers in Jesus Christ, we really are "Christian soldiers," armed with the Word of God, protected by His Spirit, and ready for a fight!

What is the most obvious manifestation of evil in your community? What might you do fight against it?

 **To Learn More**

Handbook for Spiritual Warfare by Ed Murphy

Lifeguide Bible Studies: Spiritual Warfare by Jack Kuhatscheck

Spiritual Warfare Prayers by Mark I. Bubeck

Strategy of Satan: How to Detect and Defeat Him by Warren W. Wiersbe

All additional books and resources are available from Wesleyan Publishing House at www.wesleyan.org/wph or by calling 800.4.WESLEY (800.493.7539).

Personal Spiritual Journal

DATE _____

_____

_____

_____

_____

_____

_____

_____

_____

_____

_____

_____

_____

_____

_____

My Prayer Today—

_____

_____

_____

_____

Notes

Chapter Three: A Cup of Cold Water

1. Habitat for Humanity International web site, September 13, 2002: www.habitat.org.

2. Bread for the World web site, September 13, 2002: www.bread.org.

3. UNICEF web site, September 13, 2002: www.unicef.org.

4. Senate Judicial Hearings, 1990: www.famvi.com.

5. International Labour Organization web site, September 13, 2002: www.ilo.org

6. United Nations Office for Drug Control and Crime Prevention web site, September 16, 2002: www.undcp.org.

7. National Law Center on Homelessness and Poverty cited on the Salt of the Earth web site, September 13, 2002: www.nationalhomeless.org.

8. Joni Seager, "The State of Women," *World Atlas*, 2nd ed. (New York: Penguin, 1997).

9. *Action: News from the World Association for Christian Communication*, N. 204, March 1998.

10. UNICEF web site, September 13, 2002: www.unicef.org.

11. *CIA World Factbook*, 2000, cited on the World Markets Healthcare web site, September 13, 2002: www.worldmarketsanalysis.com.

12. Johns Hopkins University Center for Communication Projects web site, September 13, 2002: www.jhuccp.org.

13. Bread for the World web site, September 13, 2002: www.bread.org.

14. IWRAW Publications web site, September 13, 2002: www.igc.org.

15. Globastat web site, September, 13, 2002: www.globastat.com.

Chapter Four: The First Shall Be Last

1. Daniel Goleman, *Working with Emotional Intelligence* (New York: Bantam Books, 1998).

2. Jim Collins, *Good to Great* (New York: Harper Collins Publishers, 2001), 20.

3. Watchman Nee, *Spiritual Authority* (New York: Christian Fellowship, 1972).

Chapter Five: God's Plan from the Beginning

1. Josh McDowell, *Right from Wrong* (Waco, Tex.: Word Publishing, 1994), 105.

2. Donald Joy, *Bonding* (Waco, Tex.: Word Books, 1985), 42.

3. H. Norman Wright, *Family is Still a Great Idea* (Ann Arbor, Mich.: Servant Publications, 1992), 17.

4. McDowell, *Right from Wrong*, 163.

5. Wright, *Family,* 90.

6. McDowell, *Right from Wrong*, 227.

7. Steve and Annie Chapman, *Married Lovers Married Friends* (Minneapolis, Minn.: Bethany House Publishers, 1989), 33.

8. Gary Chapman and Ross Campbell, *The Five Love Languages of Children* (Chicago, Ill.: Northfield Publishing, 1997), 287.

Chapter Six: Beside Still Waters

1. John Calvin, *Institutes,* I, VI, 2.

Scripture Index

Books of the Bible with Abbreviations

Old Testament

Genesis	Gen.
Exodus	Exod.
Leviticus	Lev.
Numbers	Num.
Deuteronomy	Deut.
Joshua	Josh.
Judges	Judg.
Ruth	Ruth
1 Samuel	1 Sam.
2 Samuel	2 Sam.
1 Kings	1 Kings
2 Kings	2 Kings
1 Chronicles	1 Chron.
2 Chronicles	2 Chron.
Ezra	Ezra
Nehemiah	Neh.
Esther	Esther
Job	Job
Psalms	Ps.
Proverbs	Prov.
Ecclesiastes	Eccles.
Song of Solomon	Song of Sol.
Isaiah	Isa.
Jeremiah	Jer.
Lamentations	Lam.
Ezekiel	Ezek.
Daniel	Dan.
Hosea	Hos.
Joel	Joel
Amos	Amos
Obadiah	Obad.
Jonah	Jon.
Micah	Mic.
Nahum	Nah.
Habbakuk	Hab.
Zephaniah	Zeph.
Haggai	Hag.
Zechariah	Zech.
Malachi	Mal.

New Testament

Matthew	Matt.
Mark	Mark
Luke	Luke
John	John
Acts	Acts
Romans	Rom.
1 Corinthians	1 Cor.
2 Corinthians	2 Cor.
Galatians	Gal.
Ephesians	Eph.
Philippians	Phil.
Colossians	Col.
1 Thessalonians	1 Thess.
2 Thessalonians	2 Thess.
1 Timothy	1 Tim.
2 Timothy	2 Tim.
Titus	Titus
Philemon	Philem.
Hebrews	Heb.
James	James
1 Peter	1 Pet.
2 Peter	2 Pet.
1 John	1 John
2 John	2 John
3 John	3 John
Jude	Jude
Revelation	Rev.

2 Timothy
1:7 *67*

Hebrews
12:1 *54*
12:7 *117*
13:17 *69*

James
1:2–4 *68, 117*
1:27 *94*

1 Peter
2:5, 9 *37*
2:9 *38*
3:1–12 *89*
3:7 *83, 89*
4:1 *117*
4:12–13 *117*
4:12–16 *113, 114*
5:5–6 *68*

2 Peter
1:5–7 *27*
3:9 *36*

1 John
1:5 *129*
3:16 *88*
3:17–18 *47*
4:8 *110*

Revelation
7:17 *101*

Personal Spiritual Journal

DATE _____

_____

_____

_____

_____

_____

_____

_____

_____

_____

_____

_____

_____

_____

My Prayer Today—

_____

_____

_____

_____

Personal Spiritual Journal

DATE _____

_____

_____

_____

_____

_____

_____

_____

_____

_____

_____

_____

_____

_____

_____

My Prayer Today—

_____

_____

_____

_____

Personal Spiritual Journal   DATE _____

_____

_____

_____

_____

_____

_____

_____

_____

_____

_____

_____

_____

_____

_____

My Prayer Today—

_____

_____

_____

_____

Personal Spiritual Journal

DATE _____

_____

_____

_____

_____

_____

_____

_____

_____

_____

_____

_____

_____

_____

_____

_____

My Prayer Today—

_____

_____

_____

_____

Personal Spiritual Journal

DATE _____

_____

_____

_____

_____

_____

_____

_____

_____

_____

_____

_____

_____

_____

My Prayer Today—

_____

_____

_____

_____

Personal Spiritual Journal

DATE _____

_____

_____

_____

_____

_____

_____

_____

_____

_____

_____

_____

_____

_____

_____

My Prayer Today—

_____

_____

_____

_____

Personal Spiritual Journal

DATE _____

_____

_____

_____

_____

_____

_____

_____

_____

_____

_____

_____

_____

My Prayer Today—

_____

_____

_____

_____

Personal Spiritual Journal

DATE _____

_____

_____

_____

_____

_____

_____

_____

_____

_____

_____

_____

_____

_____

My Prayer Today—

_____

_____

_____

_____

Personal Spiritual Journal

DATE _____

_____

_____

_____

_____

_____

_____

_____

_____

_____

_____

_____

_____

_____

_____

_____

My Prayer Today—

_____

_____

_____

_____

Personal Spiritual Journal

DATE _____

_____

_____

_____

_____

_____

_____

_____

_____

_____

_____

_____

_____

_____

_____

My Prayer Today—

_____

_____

_____

_____

Personal Spiritual Journal

DATE _____

_____

_____

_____

_____

_____

_____

_____

_____

_____

_____

_____

_____

My Prayer Today—

_____

_____

_____

_____

Personal Spiritual Journal

DATE _____

_____

_____

_____

_____

_____

_____

_____

_____

_____

_____

_____

_____

_____

My Prayer Today—

_____

_____

_____

_____

Personal Spiritual Journal

DATE _____

_____

_____

_____

_____

_____

_____

_____

_____

_____

_____

_____

_____

My Prayer Today—

_____

_____

_____

_____

Personal Spiritual Journal

DATE _____

_____

_____

_____

_____

_____

_____

_____

_____

_____

_____

_____

_____

_____

_____

_____

My Prayer Today—

_____

_____

_____

_____